THE SECRET DIARY

OF A

LAS VEGAS STREET MEDIC

Ty W. K. Flewelling

Copyright © 2017 Ty W.K. Flewelling

All rights reserved.

ISBN: 1978442548
ISBN-13: 978-1978442542

DEDICATION

I dedicate this book to the men and women of Mercy and American Ambulance, the Las Vegas and Clark County Fire Departments, Las Vegas Metropolitan Police Department, and the Clark County Sheriff's Department.

They are all unsung heroes!

CONTENTS

	Dedication	iii
	Preface	vii
1	Bright Lights, Big City	1
2	July Madness	19
3	Supervisors and Groids	43
4	Murder and MVA's	67
5	Work and Vacation	100
6	End of the Year Push	116
7	New Year	137
8	The Big One	157
9	The Main Event	176
10	Next Steps	208

PREFACE

I grew up on a farm in Northwest Iowa. At the age of 13, family and friends would ask me what I wanted to do when I grew up. I hadn't a clue. All I knew was that I wanted to get a job and start making my own money.

In 1978, at the age of 15, I landed my first real job that didn't involve working for a relative or family friend. The job was located on the Klingbeil Mink Farm, just south of Remsen, Iowa. The mink farm was one of approximately a dozen mink farms in the region that domestically raised tens of thousands of mink for the fur coat industry in New York. My job was simple; feed the mink, clean and change the bedding in their cages, and make "mink food" for this farm and the other mink farms in Northwest Iowa.

Simple enough, yet there were a lot of things not disclosed during the employment interview. The first being that mink are very vicious animals! They are like a cross between a wolverine and a skunk. Given the chance, they will chew a hole through your hand and spray you with a pungent liquid while doing it. It was not uncommon for mink to escape their cage and hide in the bedding between the cages. As one placed new bedding in and around the cages, mink would jump out to attack. Minor injuries were common. I quickly became the person other workers relied upon to have their cuts and mink bites cleaned and bandaged.

The job of making mink food occurred every night at 9 p.m., after the local slaughter houses closed. "Mink food" involved grinding up cow stomachs and pouring the mince into 5 pound boxes to be frozen into solid bricks, and pork lungs separated from the trachea and placed in one box with the lungs ground and boxed in a similar manner.

A second point that was never mentioned in the job interview was the fact that several of my co-workers had criminal records. It was not uncommon for the local Sheriff's department to stop by the mink farm to search employee vehicles for stolen items.

So, each night at 9 p.m., the underbelly of society would circle around a large stainless steel table, bloody knives in hand, separating pork lungs from their trachea and drinking Southern Comfort Whiskey. As the evening wore on and alcohol consumption increased, knife accuracy decreased and tempers flared. When chaos erupted, it was my job to get the hell out of the way. Once the brawlers were exhausted and bleeding, it was my job to patch them up. It was this reputation as the mink farm "medic" that kept my co-workers from tossing me into the chaos!

After several months of "medic work" on the mink farm, Glennys, a woman that worked part-time at the Mink farm and also volunteered on the local ambulance squad said, "Hey! You are pretty good at this! Have you ever thought of taking an EMT course and then volunteering on our ambulance squad?" I replied, "What's an EMT?"

She explained that an EMT was the abbreviation for an Emergency Medical Technician and was the minimum requirement needed to work on volunteer or professional ambulance squads. After taking the basic EMT course, one could take additional classes to become an EMT-Intermediate, which allowed the Technician to start IVs, use a defibrillator and place certain advanced airways. If one continued with their training, they could become a paramedic.

I grew up watching the TV shows "Squad 51" and "Emergency". Johnny Gage and Roy DeSoto were my heroes. The thought of becoming a paramedic really appealed to me. I had just turned 16 and learned that an EMT course was being offered as a night course at Western Iowa Tech Community College the following month. The course cost $500 and took three months to complete. The stickler was that you had to be 18 years old to enroll.

Being a smart and enterprising young lad. I could do the math. My application listed my date of birth as two years older! So with a $500 loan from my step-father and a slightly less than factual application, I enrolled in the Basic EMT course in the summer of 1979.

Amazingly, the Community College never asked for identification!

By September 1979, I had passed my E.M.T course and was volunteering on the Kingsley, Iowa Volunteer Ambulance Squad. I carried an Ambulance pager to High School and had the blessing from the High School Principle and Superintendent that if the pager went off, I was allowed an excused absence from school to respond to the emergency. Additionally, the squad allowed me to independently "check out" the ambulance for High School sporting events.

As a 16 year old teen, I could not believe my good fortune! While I never faked a call, there were several calls that were cancelled en route, but I never made it back to school. Additionally, I had free access to every school sporting event with reserved parking and seating. It was a brilliant set up!

Over the next year, I met members of the professional Ambulance squad, "Midwest Intercity Ambulance", in Sioux City, Iowa. They invited me to "ride along" and by the fall of 1981, I had quit working on the mink farm and was working part-time for them, part-time as an "orderly" in the St. Joseph Hospital Emergency Room and volunteering for the Emergency Services Division of the Woodbury County Sheriff's Department.

Between 1979 and 1983, I worked or volunteered on every ambulance or Sheriff Rescue shift available, all the while continuing to take paramedic courses at Western Iowa Tech. It was a wonderful time, worthy of a separate diary.

In 1983, I passed the National Registry Emergency Medical Technician – Paramedic exam and hit the streets as a fully certified street paramedic!

Shortly before my paramedic graduation, a former co-worker from Midwest Intercity Ambulance had returned to town. Ron Barnes had moved to Las Vegas, Nevada and was working for Mercy Ambulance. He regaled my co-workers and I with stories about Vegas life, the excitement of being a paramedic in "Sin City", and the fact that Mercy was hiring new graduate Paramedics. Ron thought I'd do well there and encouraged me to apply for the job.

The thought of living and working in a world-renowned city thrilled me. I applied immediately, flew down to Las Vegas two weeks later for an interview and was hired!

>	My first day on the job would be December 31, 1983.
>	New Year's Eve in Las Vegas!

Oh, one last thing…

This diary represents my reflections and opinions on life in the city of Las Vegas and while transporting patients. They are my raw thoughts as they were happening.

I'm sure others have their own 'version' of events during this time. These are mine.

1 - BRIGHT LIGHTS, BIG CITY

I have been working for Mercy ambulance for six months now. The job is extraordinary and all I had hoped it would be. I've completed my new-hire probationary period with Mercy and have been cleared for full-duty. I've also started to acclimate to life in the big city. Las Vegas is nothing like Iowa or Sioux City. It is a city that never sleeps and has all the issues that all big cities have. But if you can keep your wits about you, it is an extraordinary place to live.

The Emergency Medical Services (EMS) community was also beginning to recognize this new kid on the block, and I'm beginning to learn the names and habits of the local professionals at the Las Vegas City Fire Department, Clark County Fire Department, Las Vegas Metro Police Department, and Clark County Sheriff's Department. There are A LOT of people I needed to get to know!

The size of the EMS community was another thing that added complexity over the small EMS community I came from, and one of the reasons I chose Las Vegas.

I recently rented a house with a fellow paramedic, Jim Cox. Jim is a fit, *really large* black guy, a couple years older than me and a native of

Las Vegas. He had found a house he wanted to rent and was asking around Mercy for a roommate to split the rent. I jumped at the opportunity.

One night, just before my 21st birthday, I awoke with my heart beating fast. I was breathing heavy, and drenched in sweat. I had awoken from a nightmare. In this hellish dream were several major traumatic calls I had responded on, all blended together. They were calls that had involved shooting victims, car accidents, falls, and other traumatic injuries. They had blended together into one horrible, bloody, frightening mess. When I awoke, my senses were saturated with the smell and vision of blood. I tried to shake the vision of that horrible dream, but it never left me for the rest of the night.

The next day I was still struggling with this horrible dream. I told colleagues about it at work and they suggested that writing the calls into a diary and getting them out of my head may help. I thought that was a great idea and it became the nexus for this diary.

Tuesday, 26 June, 1984

It's 10 PM on a very hot Tuesday evening. I have just returned to Las Vegas, after visiting the folks on the family farm in Iowa. Funny, it went from 90+ % humidity in Iowa to 100+ degrees heat (and no humidity) here in Las Vegas. The temperature is still 90°F outside and it is supposed to hit 110°F tomorrow. I couldn't believe my schedule; I start a 48-hour shift Friday morning at 7 AM; Then get Sunday and Monday off work; work 24-hrs on Tuesday; Wednesday off; another 24 hrs. shift on Thursday, then Good Friday and Saturday off; then another 24 hrs. shift on Sunday. Mercy Ambulance management had me working two ambulances that Sunday, but I managed to talk them out of it by pointing out the long response times that jumping between ambulances would create. Five 24 hour shifts plus back-up call over the first 10 days back to work! I guess the guys at the company really missed me, by the time these two weeks are finished, I'll be ready for another vacation.

As I mentioned, I had returned to town from visiting the folks on the family farm in Iowa. It was my first trip back since starting work in Las Vegas and they wanted to hear about everything! When I returned to Vegas, a friend of mine, Shelley Windholtz, had collected me from the airport. Good thing Shelley drove, having just finished 10 days of vacation, sobriety was not one of my stronger points at that moment. Shelley just laughed and shook her head. Shelley is a 5'3, blonde-haired, blue-eyed native of Las Vegas and an EMT at Mercy Ambulance. For the life of me, I can't remember how we met. However it happened, we just clicked. She and I are just friends, she is in love with someone else, and I gave up on love for lust years ago! She drove me to my house and tucked me in for the night.

Wednesday, 27 June, 1984

I had every intention of tackling the backyard work, which had mysteriously aged 30 years during the 10 days I was gone. Green is my favorite color, but not when it's in my pool! Unfortunately, the hangover I was nursing was sapping my motivation. I had gotten up early, put on old clothes to get dirty in, and then looked at my waterbed and said to myself, "That looks pretty comfortable, maybe just a little nap." At noon, I woke up and proceeded to sweat my ass off in 100+ heat! While the yard looked great, I was an exhausted mess.

Thursday, 28 June, 1984

Mercy heard I was back from vacation and begged me to come in a day early. I started my first day back to work today at 7 AM with Steve Thomas. Steve is a paramedic that had been with Mercy ambulance for three years. The day went fairly smoothly except for the fact that our ambulance was a mess at the beginning of the shift! Mercy has 16 ambulances covering the city on 24 hrs. shifts at any given time. Shift changes are staggered and occur at Mercy Station 1, which is where the main administrative office and mechanic shop are located. Crews change at 6 a.m., 7 a.m., or 8 a.m. There is always a rush to get into Station 1, clean your ambulance, hand it over to the new crew and punch out. Unfortunately, some crews can be in too big of a hurry to go home that they hand over an ambulance in less than "service ready" condition. Our ambulance had no credit card for gas, the ECG telemetry Unit was dead, one of the defibrillator batteries was dead, and the ambulance was (literally) a bloody mess! Other than that the ambulance was in perfect shape. No matter what shape the ambulance, the Mercy supervisors were always 'cracking a whip' to get the ambulances (called "Units" by Mercy Dispatch) back out onto the streets and the 16 Mercy and 2 American Ambulance sub-districts covered.

Our district for the day was "sub-district three" in downtown Las Vegas. The majority of calls were alcohol-related. "I be sick", "I be pain'n", or "I done fell out" were chief amongst the complaints to be heard. Sub-district three is one of the busiest sub-districts in town. Being one of the poorer communities, this area of town is also subject to riots and violence from the local 'knife and gun club'. The area hosted a shooting at least once a week, and countless physical assaults and other forms of domestic or gang-related violence. The first call of the day came in as a "421" - woman passed out (The police radio code '421' stands for sick party). The call was strange. This 30-year-old white female, had been taking measurements for carpeting at her job site, and passed out. When she awoke, she could only remember that her name was Toni. She couldn't remember her last name, where she was, what city she was in or even how old she was. I pointed to her wedding band and asked if she was married. She stated that she didn't think she was. Upon examination, I couldn't find anything wrong; no injuries, no weakness, nothing. The only diagnosis I could come up with was a seizure of unknow etiology. We transported her to the hospital for further evaluation.

The next few calls were non-transports, just homeless bums and transients on the street looking for a place to get out of the 110°F temperature.

Our next transport was for an extremely large woman that had been involved in a motor vehicle accident. (The police radio code '401'). How this woman managed to get into the contorted position I found her in, I'll never know. In the accident, she broke both her legs. One was fractured just above the knee and wrapped around the top of the steering wheel, which she had bent forward by striking it with her chest. The other leg was broken below the knee at the mid-shin level, and was sticking out the driver's window! Her car had been sideswiped causing her to careen off the road hitting a telephone pole stabilizing wire. Now if you can imagine this 250+ pound woman, one broken leg over the steering wheel and the other out the window, in temperatures over 100°. She was sticking to the car seat and wailing in pain. I ripped my pants in three places before getting her out of the car!

After a stop by the Substation for a fresh pair of pants, our next few transports were fairly routine for a hot Vegas day. They ranged from mild over-heating to heat exhaustion and heatstroke. Fortunately, no one was in too critical a condition.

The next interesting call came in the middle of the night. After receiving the address and coordinates, I looked over at Steve and said "Head towards the Arizona-Utah border, cuz that's about where it's going to be."

Upon arrival to a small community north of the city of Las Vegas, we found a 36-year-old woman with a possible appendicitis. I started an IV and she remained stable as we transported her to the hospital. When we arrived at the hospital, I called the ambulance dispatcher and asked him if he knew where the call he had just sent us on was. He said "Yes, sort of." I told him "Well you know where the end of the world is? This call was a quarter-mile passed there!"

The rest of this first 24 hour shift was slow. Steve and I laid around our substation and rested. In this line of work, there are two golden rules: Sleep when you can and EAT when you can! Because there are shift where you will get neither! We finished our shift on time, chatted with the on-coming crew and then I went home to change clothes and come back for the next 24 hours shift.

Friday, 29 June, 1984

I started my next shift with Don Abshire in Mercy Unit 82, working out of sub-district two, which is located at Desert Springs hospital on the southeast side of Las Vegas. Don is a fantastic guy to work with. Part of what makes a good partner is being able to get along with them in between calls, and Don is first cabin in my book. Don also has a good attitude about his work. He gets pissed off at the bullshit that goes on during shift change and with middle-management, like everyone else, but he likes where he works and the working conditions. Unlike other people who do nothing but complain about having to run non-emergent calls, or calls that aren't in their district, Don just says "what the heck, it's my job." I think Don and I worked well together for having only working together a couple of times. We both believe in the same type of pre-hospital care.

The shift started off with the usual nonsense. The supervisors wanted Don to stick around for a while after the ambulance was readied for service for a meeting, but when the ambulance was ready, Don asked about the meeting and no one knew what he was talking about. Don grumbled as he got into the ambulance and we left.

The Unit had only one set of keys. When the off-going crew was asked where the other set of keys were they replied "Oh, this ambulance has only had one set of keys for some time now." And so it went for most of the morning. I said to Don as we finally pulled away from the station, "You know Don, today could really turn into an inconvenience". Don just shook his head.

The first transport of the day came just as we pulled into the key shop to get the second set of keys made for our ambulance. The call was a bedridden, elderly woman at home with a urinary tract infection that needed non-emergent transportation to Sunrise Hospital. (Put into ambulance parlance - a "Code 2" call). The woman only had mild discomfort and would have been pretty routine except for the fact that the hall to her bedroom was narrow and we had to carry her out to our stretcher. Don and I are trained to do this, which was no problem. The problem arose when we placed her on the stretcher. The latch which holds the stretcher at different levels didn't fully latch and fell all the way to the floor. Luckily the elderly woman was uninjured; startled but okay. Don just smiled and looked at the woman and said in a very professional manner, "Don't worry ma'am, you are the first person I've dropped all week, but I always catch them on the very first bounce!" As we lifted the gurney up again, I looked at Don and said "It's got to get better, we've already hit worse." The rest of the call was uneventful, and the patient made it to the hospital in one piece, and alive.

Upon going back 10-8 into service (meaning ready for another call) from Sunrise hospital, our next response was to Bullhead city hospital to pick up a post-heart attack patient and transport him back to Valley Hospital in Las Vegas. This call became screwed up as well. I swear some days nothing goes right!! Originally, Unit 90, A Basic Life Support (BLS) Unit was dispatched to take the transfer. Unit 90 was halfway there, when Bullhead City decided they needed a Paramedic Unit instead of a Basic EMT Unit, so we were sent. Bullhead city is approximately 85 miles from Las Vegas, and Unit 90 had gone about 40 miles outside of the city limits before they were canceled. Don and I thought this was just great. We radioed en route to Bullhead with dispatch, then pulled into a 7-Eleven store, grabbed a couple of cokes and headed off on our "Sunday drive" to Bullhead city hospital.

Mercy ambulance has a substation in Laughlin Nevada, which is just across the river from Bullhead city, Arizona. The Ambulance crews on duty in Laughlin are only Basic Life Support certified. To say that Laughlin Nevada is small would be an understatement. Laughlin was almost a Ghost town until several casinos decided to make a major investment in the town. Suddenly, a small town sprung up to support casino construction. If you stood on one end of town and threw a rock to the other end of town, you'd only have to walk 100 yards to pick the rock up again. Well maybe it's not that small, but it only has three streets. As Don and I drove into Bullhead city, I looked at Don and asked "Do you know where the hospital is?" He looked at me and said, "Hell no, I thought you did". We looked around for a while and couldn't find it, so we drove back across the river to the Mercy substation and asked the crew on duty. Dan Netski, one of the senior Mercy supervisors, was in Laughlin helping get the Ambulance sub-station going, and he told us where the hospital was located. Real convenient...The hospital was three miles outside of town and not close to anything!

Dan chatted with Don and I for a few minutes. It seemed things hadn't been too much fun for him here. Some of the local personnel in the Sub-station are real "desert geeks", extremely green and too cocky for their own good. Additionally, the Bullhead city fire department had their feathers all ruffled thinking Mercy ambulance was going to take over their jobs in Bullhead city.

We headed to the hospital and collected our patient and returned to Las Vegas. It was a long and boring ride. We returned to town at around 3 p.m. to watch Las Vegas get its first rain of the year, as well as its first floods of the year. It rained cats and dogs! And cows and sheep and everything else! Every street we tried to take was flooded. In Nevada, you never cross a flooded road, even if it only looks a few inches deep. Flash floods can cut through a road and those few inches of water can turn out to be several feet deep. Drive into it and you are dead! Fortunately, we found a clear path and made it to the hospital.

We had just cleared Valley Hospital when we received a call for a man who had fallen. When we arrived on scene we found a cantankerous old coot that had slipped, fallen and broken his hip. He called us everything but a good milk cow, and we had just gotten there! This sort of attitude upset Don, but I thought he was kind of funny. Since this was Don's patient, I retrieved all the equipment for him and sat back and watched Don and this guy argue. The old guy was convinced that Don was part of some neo-Nazi youth group and Don was positive that the old guy was a senile, old asshole! Through all the fuss, we finally managed to stabilize him onto the stretcher, placed into the ambulance and transport him to the hospital.

The better portion of the late afternoon and early evening were filled with false starts and bogus calls. We did transport a gentleman that had gotten into some bad cabbage and was convinced that the heartburn he was feeling was a heart attack and that he was going to die. During transport to the hospital, after a hearty burp, his heartburn suddenly went away – another miracle cure!

All in all, this shift went fairly well. Enough calls to say we did something, but not enough to say we were overworked.

7 AM Saturday, 30 June, 1984

Saturday morning rolled around and Don and I rolled back into Mercy's main headquarters, Station 1, to clean our Unit and transfer it to the on-coming crew. I punched my time card and headed home, showered and was back to work for my third 24hr. shift at 8:30 a.m. on American Ambulance - "Medic 2". American Ambulance was recently purchased by Mercy ambulance and catered to the more affluent neighborhoods of Las Vegas. While a few paramedics work strictly for one or the other service, most paramedics bounce back and forth between the blue Mercy Ambulance uniform and the light brown American Ambulance one. I am working with Cliff Mitchell today, a part-time paramedic for both Mercy and American ambulance companies. Cliff worked full-time for the Clark County Fire Department as a paramedic. He had been doing this for about seven years, and had an attitude of "do whatever you want to do, I don't care as long as it works." Cliff is a pretty decent guy to work with, he just puts in his time and doesn't try to change the world. As usual, we went through the morning harassments of restocking, getting appropriate equipment, and listening to middle management propaganda. Then we were off, ready to stamp out lives and save disease – *the model of socialized medicine to keep all medical professionals in business.*

The morning was fantastic, only one call for a 35-year-old female that was in a swimming pool, trying to catch her daughter as she slid down the slide. Mom missed her catch, and her daughter nailed her in the face with both feet. I don't know if the little girl did it on purpose or if mom was just klutzy enough to stand right in front of the slide. Anyway, mom earned a trip to the hospital.

I find it odd, people all over the world save and save to take a vacation in Las Vegas, but when they finally get here, they do something stupid the very first day in town. Far too often the minute people get into town, they go non-stop until they drop, spending only a day on the strip, and the rest of the time recuperating in a hospital. I wonder if people think the town is going to close up at midnight?

Others are too busy looking at the pretty lights and then walk onto the street in front of cars or drive into something within minutes of getting into town. Countless times I've heard, "we drove clear from Detroit Michigan without any problems, then this happens." I usually say, "Long way to go just to have an accident don't you think?"

Then there are those, that no matter what, they are going on vacation. It doesn't matter to them that they are having chest pain or can't breathe. They saved up for this trip and they are going to Vegas to have fun! Sadly, many of these tourists go home in a box.

As the day wore on, and the thunderclouds started to build, so did the calls. I was told at the end of this 12 hour period, Mercy ambulance had transported over 150 patients.

Our chaos started with a 94-year-old female experiencing difficulty breathing. Upon our arrival, the fire department said, "Oh, she's got some problems breathing, but she's okay." I went into the apartment and found a little lady laying in a bed with audible wheezes that I could hear from the door! Upon listening to her lungs with the stethoscope, I heard lots of wheezing, rales, and rhonchi. (In layman's terms, lots of junk) I looked back at the firemen and said, "She's not as okay as you think, let's put her on some oxygen. I'm going to call in for orders." The firemen grumbled, but did what I asked. I received orders to place her on O2, start an IV of D5W, administer Lasix and to transport.

We had just placed a patient on the emergency room stretcher when we received a call for a 401 (auto accident). Halfway to the accident, we were canceled and rerouted to a different call. Halfway to the second call we were again canceled and sent to a third call, and were canceled just as we pulled onto the scene of that call! I'm sure people thought we were crazy rushing back and forth with red lights and siren, but never ever getting anywhere.

With a lull in the action, we worked to catch up on our paperwork from previous calls and then headed back to our substation. Emergency calls slowed down for a little while, long enough for us to watch the movie "From 10 to Midnight". A crime-horror-thriller starring Charles Bronson. Ironically, our next call was for a shooting at the Maxim hotel. It seems that our patient caught someone trying to steal things from his car, and during the scuffle was shot in the leg by the thief with a .38 caliber pistol. Our patient said that he didn't even hear the shot. He had recovered from polio in that leg, so he didn't even feel it. He related that he just looked down and saw blood, so he called for help. When we took his polio splint off his leg to bandage the wound, the bullet fell out. Seems that the bullet went through his leg but didn't have enough force to go through the splint. We bandaged his leg and headed for the hospital.

I was the driver for this call and as I looked to the north, while driving east on flamingo Road, the Las Vegas Hilton was covered by what looked like a rain cloud. Then the wind hit us followed by the dust. It was a huge dust storm and visibility dropped to almost zero! I thought to myself, drop the temperature and change the dust to snow and this would be a blizzard!

The rain followed the dust and with it the call volume soared. Our next call was to Rose De Lima Hospital in Henderson Nevada. Upon our arrival, we were informed that we were going to be transporting a patient to Southern Nevada Memorial. The patient was believed to have an intracranial bleed, was unconscious, and with decorticate posturing (an abnormal posturing in which the patient is stiff with bent arms, clenched fists, and legs held out straight.). Our patient had three strikes against him before we even left for Southern Memorial Hospital (So. Ma. Mo. hospital in street slang.) I learned from the transferring nurse that his problems started at noon today and it was now 11:30 PM. The Rose De Lima emergency room staff weren't sure what he initially had, but had infused a liter of lactated ringers into him before they finally decided he had an intracranial bleed. The added fluid caused the patient to go into congestive heart failure with pulmonary edema and tragically they had done nothing to try and lower his temperature which was above 100°F. After we had loaded the patient into the ambulance, I radioed ahead and informed So. Ma. Mo. that we were in route with the nice patient from the good people at Rose De Lima. The man will probably have permanent brain damage, along with secondary heart problems due to the ignorance of the few nurses, if he survived at all.

The rain came down and the streets turned into rivers. Of course, everyone had to go somewhere! It was like rush hour traffic all over again! Our next call was to the intersection of Spring Mountain Rd. and Polaris street for a three-car pileup. An intoxicated driver ran the red light and hit another car which in turn hit a third car. As we arrived on scene, I turned my attention to a 20-year-old male that was laying stretched out in the backseat of the intoxicated driver's vehicle. Joey was his name. I asked him where he was hurting, he replied that his right shoulder was really bothering him. A first responder had already bandaged the shoulder in a sling. I asked him if he hurt anywhere else, to which he replied "No". As I continued my assessment, I discovered that Joey could not move his legs nor could he feel anything from the nipple line down. Joey was definitely hurting far worse than he even realized.

Sadly, I determined that Joey was paralyzed from the nipple line down. I carefully extracted him from the car and placed him on a spine board, and then into the ambulance. While I was getting Joey ready to be moved, the intoxicated driver of the vehicle was giving the other medics a hard time, saying "I don't want any of you fucking people to touch me, I'm okay, and so is Joey. Why don't you people just leave us the fuck alone." I turned around with fire in my eyes and said, "Joey is going to the hospital, because Joey isn't feeling well right now! Joey can't move his legs nor feel anything anymore because of your fucking driving, and if you know what's best for you, you'll keep your damn mouth shut and let the paramedics take care of you!" We then took Joey to the hospital where I later found out that he had transacted his spinal cord at C7. Poor guy, it just wasn't his day. First, he got into the wrong car with the wrong person and ended up getting into an accident, then after having been sat up, so as to make it easy to wrap his shoulder injury, the first responders paralyzed him for life. LIFE!!! That's a long time not to be able to feel again, run again. All Joey's goals and dreams, washed away.

When I was 17, I also got into the vehicle of an intoxicated driver. That mistake resulted in a high speed chase by Iowa Highway Patrol and local law enforcement. The driver ended up hitting a telephone pole at 70 miles per hour. He broke his nose, but I suffered a compacted fracture of my lower spine and had to wear a back brace for 6 months. I was lucky. I could have ended up like Joey. My experience motivated me to speak at local High Schools in Iowa and now Las Vegas of the dangers of drinking and driving. Sometimes I wonder, however, whether anyone will listen. How many will suffer. People never think things like this will happen to them. I'm sure Joey never imagined it either. People can be so foolish. They waste their lives on stupid chances. Things they could avoid. My experience has caused me to believe that there is a difference between social fantasy and reality, and cases like this confirm my beliefs. People live in a buffer zone that is just wide enough to be comfortable, trying to live out the fantasy they see on TV, yet the fantasy is only a fantasy and doesn't deal with the realities of the world and the way things really happened. People come to Vegas and think the rules of the real world no longer apply. Sadly, they apply more here than back on the farm where life can be a bit more forgiving. I think this is one of the reasons why paramedics are a breed all to their own. We have to live between the social fantasy and reality and it's not easy. It's hard for people outside our field to understand us, you have to experience what we do. The job stress factor is high, burnout is high and personal relationships suffer tremendously. So why do we do what we do? The honest answer is for the thrill, but it is also very personally rewarding.

The rest of the evening was filled with more accidents, drunks slipping on wet casino floors, a guy that had his car repossessed and when he tried to stop them, was soundly pummeled into the dirt. Those repo guys are goons!

The evening wore on and the next thing we knew it was morning and the calls still kept coming. I was never so glad to see 8:30 AM, and be able to go home and sleep! Poor Cliff was doing two back-to-back 24 hr. shifts in the same ambulance. I smiled and waved to him as he headed back out on to the street for his next call.

8:30 AM Sunday, 1 July, 1984

It was the start of my two days off and boy was I looking forward to it. Upon arriving home I left a trail of clothes into the bedroom. As I got into bed the phone started ringing, I thought to myself, "Self, I'll answer the phone this time, but after that it's coming unplugged." It was Paramedic Cliff Mitchell, who begged and pleaded until I finally agreed to work for him at 10 PM that night. I hung up and unplugged the phone and became unconscious until 5:30 in the evening. Shelley came over and invited me to her house for dinner. Not being one to turn down free food, I graciously accepted. Shelley's sister makes fantastic spaghetti. While I was there, several of Shelley's relatives came over and one of her uncles who had an unnatural hatred of Texans reminded me of the joke one of my partners told me. It goes like this:

> *There once was this guy, that just couldn't stand Texans. Just hated their guts. He even had a T-shirt that said, "Texans are the stupidest damn people in the whole world." Well anyway this guy had to take a trip to Mexico and had to go through Texas. While stepping in a small Texas town, he walked into a bar, looked at the bartender and said, "Pour me a beer you stupid, ugly, son of a bitch!" The bartender leaned over the bar and said, "I ain't going to give you a beer and you can't wear that T-shirt in my bar." Well they went round and round and finally stepped out back to settle it once and for all. The bartender whipped out a switchblade knife that glistened in the sun and was razor-sharp, but the traveler just laughed. The bartender looked at him in a fury and said, "what the hell you laughing at?!" The traveler replied, "just like a stupid Texan to bring a knife to a gunfight!"*

Well, Shelley thought it was funny. Shelley and I jumped into my Pontiac Fierro and drove around town until I had to go back to work. She gave me a hard time about being a workaholic, which I couldn't really argue with. The truth was, I loved doing what I do more than anything else.

I clocked back in at 10:15 p.m. to start work with Robin Nunn. Robin and Cliff came into the office with a worried look on their faces and asked me if I knew where the electrode cable was for the ECG monitor. It seems that they had gone all day without realizing it was missing. I told them that I thought it was in the ambulance. I told Cliff that after our last monitor patient, I had taken the cables off of the patient, rolled it up and put it on our gurney to be put away while I did the paperwork. Cliff thought someone had taken them. I said, "No worries, I'll find a spare set until we locate the original ones. In the meantime, you'd better notify the supervisor on duty and let him know. It is better he finds out from us than someone else." John Stanton was the supervisor on duty and sleeping in his on-call room. Needless to say he was not happy to be awakened or to discover that he now needed to go track down missing equipment!

I found a spare set of monitor cables and we were back in business. I was again working on American Ambulance Medic Two. Fortunately, the shift had slowed down, only two calls the entire night. The first call was for an attempted suicide via overdose of multiple medications. It wouldn't have killed her, but she did get the attention she wanted. The nurses at the hospital gave her their undivided attention for a whole hour as they pumped her stomach. The final call was a 401 (motor vehicle accident) involving two cars. We transported two patients to the hospital with lacerations on their face and complaining of neck and back pains. Both were stable with minimal discomfort.

Then, the moment Robin and I had been waiting for, the end of shift and the "Wrath of Stanton." Robin explained to John what had happened with the cables, but John blamed me! I was pissed. He told me that if we didn't find them that I was going to have to buy a new set of cables. I found this outrageous. If my ambulance had been stolen, would I have to buy a new ambulance? Hell no! It wasn't my fault that the cables were missing. On a call, the driver cleans up and the attendant does the paperwork. Cliff was responsible for getting all the equipment back into the rig.

As I was fuming, Mercy Unit 84 pulled up and said we've got an extra set of monitor cables in our rig is anybody missing this? I said, " Mr. Stanton. Your cables." I then walked into the station, punched out and went home. Man was I upset.

8:30 AM Monday, 2 July, 1984

I arrived home, changed clothes, and was heading to bed when the phone rang; it was dispatch asking if I wanted to be on call. After unloading on the poor dispatcher about "Cable-gate", I felt sorry and said "okay." I then dressed, and drove back down to the station to pick up my pager. On the way back home with my pager, I remembered that I needed to stop by the Clark County Credit Union to cash a check to have money for the week. I then went home and raked the backyard to let off steam. My pool was still green. Time for heavy chemical warfare. After cleaning the yard and fixing the pool it was time to take a shower. I had just stepped out of the shower when my pager went off. It was 1 o'clock in the afternoon. So back to work I went. I hadn't eaten all day, so I asked Dale Netski, who was on call with me, if he had eaten. He hadn't either. So first order of business was food!

As misfortune would have it, we received a call before we made it to the restaurant. The call was for a woman that couldn't stand. We arrived on scene and found that her apartment door was locked. The manager finally came along and opened the door. Inside, we found an elderly woman lying on the floor of her living room. After examining her, we determined she was a diabetic with a dangerously low blood sugar. Her doctor called her house and asked that she be transported to Rose De Lima Hospital. Since Dale and I were the on-call crew in a BLS ambulance (with no ACLS equipment), the Las Vegas Rescue paramedics had to ride with us to the Henderson hospital. We started an IV and pushed an ampule of D 50 W. By the time we arrived to the hospital in Henderson, our patient was awake and alert.

After we had finished the call, we quickly grabbed a bite to eat from a near-by fast food joint. I was also able to pick up additional chemicals for my pool! I punched back out at Station 1 and went home at 6:30 PM. After attacking the pool, I bummed around the house until lights out at 11 PM.

2 - JULY MADNESS

8:30 AM Tuesday, 3 July, 1984

My workday started in the usual manner. There was chaos as the night crews arrived late for shift-change and the oncoming crews worked quickly to restock their rigs and prepared for the day. Apparently, the departing shift had had a very busy night and hadn't had time to restock all that well. In fact, upon checking our ambulance, the stock was so depleted that I figured they must have been giving stuff away in addition to what they had used! Getting ready for service took a while and the supervisors complained because we weren't on the streets "stomping out lives and saving disease." It all went in one ear and out the other. What are they going to do to me? Take away my birthday?

We were on the street by 9:15 AM. I thought that was fast enough. Our first call of the day was an emergency response to Rose De Lima hospital in Henderson, NV for a 12-year-old girl that was throwing premature ventricular contractions (PVCs). Upon connecting the heart monitor I found she was actually in trigeminy! (Trigeminy is where the heart is throwing irregular heartbeats (PVCs) after every third beat.) During this transport, I chatted with the patient about her history. The longer we talked, it became clear that she had had this problem for quite some time and that her old docs never followed up. Fortunately, she remained stable and was an extremely pleasant patient, all bubbly and cheerful.

Our next call came just as we dropped this young girl off at So. Ma. Mo hospital. A MVA (motor vehicle accident) at the intersection of Nellis and Tropicana Boulevard. Rescue 14 was there with my good friend Riley Peeples. Not to try and cut Riley down or anything (that would be impossible, Riley would have to approve before he could be cut down any further), but Riley was once again out to lunch. He didn't want to put a Kendricks Extrication Device (KED Board) on an unrestrained, injured lady for spinal precautions, he didn't take any vital signs, I don't think he even did a proper patient assessment! I said, "That's okay Riley, Robin and I will get all that useless assessment stuff in our ambulance. Meanwhile how about humoring me by allowing us to put her on the KED board and place there on a long backboard? Just for tickles and grins of course. Well Riley didn't know, but he thought it would probably be all right. (What a twit!!) We managed to keep Riley from hurting, I mean helping anyone and loaded the women into our ambulance. I quickly locked the door to keep Riley from climbing in behind.

Luckily, our patient didn't speak much English and didn't really know what was being said or going on. We had just transported her to Desert Springs hospital when we received our next call for another motor vehicle accident at the intersection of Tropicana and Koval. Fortunately, Riley was nowhere in sight. The woman on scene wasn't hurt that badly, but she sure wanted to hurt the person that hit her! She swore like a longshoreman. I picked up three new curse words from her! I don't think they had any real meaning, but they sure sounded disgusting and wicked.

As the day wore on, we ran a few more inter-hospital transfers; a woman that had taken an overdose of antibiotics, (we figured she wouldn't get an infection until the year 1993!); A guy injured in a bicycle accident that had been broadsided by an RV; and the usual run-of-the-mill intoxicated family members vomiting their guts out on the living room floor and alarming the rest of the family into calling an ambulance.

The wee hours of the morning appeared to be our time for rest. We returned to our substation at around 1 AM and went to sleep. We were blessed with 2 ½ full hours of sleep before responding to an assault victim at 3:30 in the morning. What we found was a slightly melodramatic transgender person that had gotten smacked in the nose. I found him/her laying on the living room floor moaning and groaning, the fire department engine crew said that they had checked him/her out and couldn't find anything other than a bloody nose, which had stopped bleeding some time ago. The patient's name was Mark, so I knelt down beside him and asked, "What's the matter Mark?" "Are you hurting anywhere?" He moaned back, "I can't breathe". I said, "Well you look like you're breathing okay to me Mark. Do you hurt anywhere?" Mark then started to hyperventilate and stammered, "The lower lobe of my left lung collapsed and I'm keeping it inflated through hypnotic powers". I said, "Oh... Sounds pretty serious... So you want to go to the hospital, or do you think you've got everything under control?" He then started yelling for his mother, he's 30 years old! And his mother is in California! I said, "Enough of this B. S. ! I'm not waiting any longer, if you want to go to the hospital, fine! Let's get going, but I'm not going to stand here and listen to you scream for your mother!" Mark says, "Okay let's go." I said, "Okay give me your hand and I'll help you up". Mark said, "Carry me". The things that ran through my mind when this little Queenie said that, were like none I've ever thought of before while on a call. But I kept my composure and said, "No dice chump, you walk down to the ambulance or you don't go." I withdrew my hand and said, "And you get up on you own". I then started walking for the door. Mark then started crawling for the door begging me to please help him. The Las Vegas police officers were in tears laughing so hard. I said, "Oh for Pete's sake, get on your feet and quit acting like an invalid." Mark then grabbed the door and very dramatically started pulling himself up. I said, "I thought you didn't hurt your legs?" Mark said, "I didn't". I said, "Then why are you acting like both your legs are broken!" He said, "Oh", then properly rose to his feet and walked down to the ambulance with me as if nothing had happened.

I placed Mark on the gurney and he started going into his "I can't breathe" act again. I then lost it. I said, "Now you knock this bull shit off right here and now! You are going to answer my questions otherwise I'm going to throw you out on your ass!" Miraculously, Mark was able to talk again. He looked up at me with a mean look and said in a stern queenie voice, "You don't believe me do you?" I retorted back in the same queenie voice, "No I don't". We argued back and forth for a while, and then he faked unconsciousness, so I broke an ammonia capsule under his nose, which started him gagging. I said, "Not as unconscious as you thought you were?" And then chuckled. When we arrived to the hospital, I told the ER staff what my patient had related to me and laughed as I left the emergency department.

The rest of the night was uneventful. Thank God! I don't think I could've managed many more "Marks" in the same evening.

10 PM 12 July, 1984

How time flies when you're working your tail off. I've lost track as to how many calls I've run since I last wrote. The time is 11:45 PM and I've had only one and a half days off since July 3rd . I'm tired. I'm grumpy. I really need some down time. Lately, it just doesn't seem worth all the effort being put forth. Sixty percent of the patients are jerks or transients that don't care what they do or whose home they bother. I sometimes feel like they think that's their purpose in life to make others miserable. Add to this the fact that three paramedics are on vacation and three have quit and two more have indicated that they are also going to leave.

The staff shortages are making the work load and stress laid on the rest of us unbearable. The city is packed with conventioneers. Everything from electronics to the fabric industry. People are everywhere, traffic is impossible, and everyone feels that their agendas are more important than those of anyone else. The calls have been as diverse as the people; from a Mexican dignitary having a heart attack to the 15-year-old pregnant teenager having labor pains, and just about everything else in between that you can imagine.

Going back over some of the more interesting calls.

Man, thinking back, it was the week for beating up your wife! We had several calls where the husband's daily routine before going to work was; getting up in the morning, taking a shower, eating breakfast, reading the paper, slapping the wife and kids around for an hour, then heading to work.

I don't know why these women put up with B. S. like this. I asked a couple of them and all they could answer was "I don't know where I'd go." This sense of helplessness resulted in several trying to kill themselves. I related to one of them, "My God, woman! Don't you think your husband is abusing you enough? Then to have you started in on yourself also?! Are you going to leave your kids to that asshole all alone?"

I also had a few really nice patients that appreciated me being there. We had a 23-year-old guy that rolled his pickup and was ejected, skidding down the street on his side. He suffered copious amounts of 'road rash' to his right arm and shoulder. He was really hurting. He told me he was a boxer and had won a few Golden Globe championships, and never had anything hurt so bad. We gave him extra T.L.C. and he really appreciated it. Which lifted my dog-ass tired spirits at 3 AM.

I've come to the conclusion that people like myself are put on this earth to babysit everybody else. Some of the profound statements people make are simply unreal! The other day, while working on American Ambulance - M2 with Robin Nunn, I responded to a call at the Tropicana Hotel where a man was complaining of severe abdominal pain. The patient stated that he had a PhD and was a "Dr." He was no more a medical doctor than my ceramic dog "Spot" was a dog. He gave us this big story and told us he thought it was a dissecting aortic aneurysm. He had an aneurysm like I'm the Pope! He insisted on going to the hospital, so I said "Sure." I figured we'd give him a $200 ambulance bill and make him feel like a total idiot in the emergency room when he found out there was nothing wrong with him.

We secured him to our cot, loaded him into the ambulance and headed off for Desert Springs hospital. The man's girlfriend was riding along in the front seat and I attempted to make idle conversation while in route - It was like talking to a tomato! During our chit chat she relates, "Golly Las Vegas is a lot bigger than I thought it would be." I said, "600,000." She said, "What? Square feet?" I looked at her in total amazement and said "No...people." Needless to say the conversation stopped abruptly.

It's uncanny, when paramedics get tired and start to burnout, they start messing with their patients' minds. Another crew told me the story about two PCP (an animal tranquilizer) drug addicts they had transported. One of the PCP'ers had passed out and been placed on the cot. The crew was about to depart the scene with just the one patient, because the second PCP patient had refused treatment. Just as they were ready to drive away, they heard yelling and saw the Metro police officers beating the heck out of the second PCPer. The police opened the back door of the ambulance and threw the half-conscious second PCPer on the squad bench and then the Metro police officer jumped in to the ambulance to ride along.

As the second PCPer regained his wits, he looked up at the Metro police officer and said, "Shit man, you going to kill me?" The Metro police officer said, "No. You're already dead." Pointing to the man on the stretcher he said, "This man over here was robbing the gas station and you got mouthy with him, so he shot you in the head! You're dead! Then I shot him in the head and his buddy shot me. We are all three dead." Then the police officer looked over at the paramedic writing his report in the jump seat and said, "And this here is an 'Angel of Mercy', he's come to take us to heaven." The second PCPer then became emotional and started to bawl. "Oh no man, I can't be dead. Oh no!" Both the Metro police officer and the paramedic kept it up all the way to the hospital. It definitely helped relieve the monotony of the day, plus gives one a good story to tell the other medics.

Oh Lord, I can't even think straight anymore. It's 1 AM, I'm going to bed.

Sadly, I never got the chance to get in bed. Just as I was sitting on the edge of the bed, my partner and I received another call. It is now 2:15 AM and it was a call that just tore us apart.

The call came in as a child not breathing. My partner and I quickly dressed and headed for the ambulance. With the sleep still in our eyes, I started the engine and Robin grabbed the microphone to put us in route. The dispatcher came over the radio, "Medic two, 421, child not breathing." We found the district and phantom numbers (a system for quickly locating an address in the city) in our map book, and headed for the address. The address put the call about six miles from our substation. We knew that rescue would probably beat us to the scene. Traffic was light and we made good time getting to the call. As we pulled up, we noticed that Rescue had only taken their jump box, so Robin grabbed all our equipment and headed for the apartment. A Metro police officer had pulled in behind us and asked me if I thought he was needed. I told him the call came in as a child not breathing, and that he could come up if he wanted. He did.

Robin entered the dimly lit room ahead of me. As I entered the room, I saw a small child, five or six years old, laying on the floor motionless and very cyanotic (blue). I looked around for an oxygen cylinder but saw none. I immediately spun around, raced back to my ambulance, grabbed our 02 cylinder and ran back as quickly as I could.

As I reentered the room, Robin looked up at me and shook her head. We were just too late to do anything. The mother still hadn't realized what had happened, so we took her into a side room to ask a few questions as to what had happened. She related to us the story of a fantastic little boy, so active and full of life. Never being sick or having any problems at birth. She related that the boy's uncle had visited earlier in the evening and he and the child had talked about everything under the sun, and had related, just before going to bed, "my stomach hurts, but Mommy I love you and I'm going to go to bed now."

At around Midnight his mother noticed that he had vomited and had gone limp. Then 1/2 hour later he started to turn blue. His mother then looked at my partner and I and asked, "He's going to be all right, isn't he?" There was a long pause and then Robin said "I'm very sorry but I'm afraid there is nothing we can do for your son, he's gone." The little boy's mother fell apart screaming "No, I don't believe you!" and ran back into the room where the lifeless little body lay. The boy's mother collapsed by his side, crying uncontrollably, and sobbing "Why? Why? He was such a good little boy, he never hurt anyone. Why him? Why!" After a few minutes, the Metro police officer and I escorted her back into the kitchen. One of the Fire Department paramedics had to leave the room. The emotions were just too much. He had a little boy a year younger than this one. As he was stepping out of the room, I said, "you guys can go 10-8 (back into service), we'll wait for the corner."

Robin followed the Fire Department guys out to the ambulance to make sure they were all right and to try and talk out the call a little. I sat down with the boy's mother in the kitchen and tried to help her cope. I knew it would be impossible, but I had to try. She looked at me with tears running down her face and asked me, "Why did he die? How could this have happened? He's never been sick before at all." I answered, "I really wish I knew, more than likely he probably had something wrong since birth and it just now showed itself. I sincerely wished we could have saved him. You don't know how deeply sorry I am." Her uncle came over and embraced her. She looked up at him and said, "He was all that I had." He said, "I know." I walked over to the Metro officer and said, "I think we'll take off if you can handle everything. Please give us a call back if you think she needs to be taken to the hospital for counseling and support." The Metro officer said "I think I'll be all right. I'll call you back if you're needed." I said solemnly, "Thanks. See you later." I headed for the ambulance and met Robin halfway. I said, "Let's go. I can't handle anymore." As we were walking back to the ambulance, Robin told me that Jim (the Fire Department paramedic) was taking it pretty rough. "I don't think he's going to get much sleep tonight," she said. "I don't think he'll be the only one." I responded.

We boarded our ambulance and advised dispatch we were 10-8 (available), and that the patient was 419 (dead). The drive back to the substation was silent, each of us thinking about the beautiful boy that would no longer be, and about how I wished that I could educate parents and relatives to take basic first aid courses. If only we could have been there sooner, if only the boy's mother had realized there was a problem. If only...

God, I wanted to resuscitate that kid. I wanted to try so bad that I could taste it. But I knew there was no hope. The ECG was flatlining, his pupils were fixed and dilated, his skin was cyanotic, and lividity (the setting of blood) was already starting to occur. Three plus strikes, our patient was out. Game over. Out for the season. Out for life.

Robin and I arrived back to the substation and I was desperate for sleep. But all I could do was think about the boy and his family. We received another call for an assault victim and after dropping him off at Sunrise hospital, Robin asked me "Where to next?" I said, "I don't care. I can't sleep, how about Desert Springs? Let's see what they are up to." Robin said, "Sounds good to me."

We never did get any sleep for the rest of the shift. We kept getting call after call after call, which was just as well. It kept us from thinking about the boy too much.

I was beyond tired at 1 AM and here I am at 7 AM. I'm still awake and functioning. Life on a 24 hour shift revolves around the ability to get little "cat naps." It is amazing how a 15-minute nap can boost you just enough to get by. But there are days when one doesn't get any sleep. I hated those days! I get this numbness between my eyes, and a fog over my brain.

There have been times when I have fallen in an exhausted heap on the substation bed and went immediately to sleep, only to be awakened 10 minutes later for a call. The body knows it has to get up and move (what I call impulse mode) but the brain lags behind. I remember responding to a call (as the driver) and while driving down the road, only then fully waking up behind the wheel and having to ask my partner, "Where are we going?" It's crazy!

Eight AM came and our shift was over. I made a beeline for home and my waterbed. Emotional stress or no emotional stress, I needed sleep.

But of course, I was still on call.

8:30 AM Friday, 13 July, 1984

Upon arriving home, I shed everything but my pants and went out to skim the swimming pool. Then went to sleep. An hour later the phone rang. It was Shelley, "What you doing?" I said, "Guess." She said, "You're not sleeping are you?" I replied, "All day long!" She started talking and about an hour later I woke up again and hung up the phone. Shelley is a champ and deserving of more attention that she is getting from me, but I really needed to sleep. Just before rolling over and going back to sleep, I thought to myself, "I'm not going to answer that phone again today." So the phone came unplugged from the wall and I slept until 4:30 PM.

At that time, I heard a knock on my bedroom patio door. It was Shelley. "Had enough sleep yet?" "I haven't decided," I replied. She came in and we talked for a while. I finally woke up and got out of bed. I had literally plugged my phone back into the wall and it rang. It was dispatch. "We're busy, can you come in right away?" I said, "I'll be right in." Shelley just laughed and said, "Will you put me down as the beneficiary in your will when you die?"

Pete Vier was the other paramedic on-call. He had been poolside most of the afternoon and his hair was still wet as he arrived to Station 1. Pete is in his late 20s, rusty-blonde hair, and would easily fit the role of a Life Guard on any TV show. We jumped into an ambulance and took off for the busy end of town. We didn't run any calls, but chatted with a lot of pretty girls. I had promised Teresa Howell (a Mercy Administrative Clerk) that I would take her to a movie and so at 6 PM, when I got off call, I called her up and said, "You ready?" She said, "Yes", so off to the movies we went. Teresa is one of three Mercy Admin girls that belongs to 'The Breakfast Club' (A group of Mercy employees that tend to do social functions together.) "Gremlins" was a pretty good flick, even when you're dog-ass tired.

At around midnight I dropped Teresa off at her house and then headed over to Sunrise hospital. I had promised some of the ER nurses that I would drive by and show them my car. After chatting with them for a while, I dragged my butt home at 1 AM to get some sleep before starting a 48 hour shift at 8 AM that morning.

God, I need another vacation!

8 AM Saturday, 14 July, 1984

Friday the 13th came and went and I didn't turn into a gremlin. However, this morning I do feel like a zombie! I'm working with Mike Sherwood today. Mike is today's shift supervisor. Oh boy! (Sarcasm) Mike is a... Well,... What I mean to say is... Mike is!

I probably shouldn't be so hard on him, but if I didn't, somebody else would, so what the hell! The morning started well. Only one call, and that was for "Mr. Secks", which sounded like "Mr. Sex." It was very hard to take the man seriously. He was a senile 70-year-old man that didn't want to go to the hospital.

The rest of the day ran smoothly as well. Mike and I actually got along fantastically. We talked about everything from ambulance work to the crazy things we both had done in the past. At the end of the shift, I had to laugh. All the patients that I took care of were mild mannered and well-behaved, whereas all the patients that Mike took care of were crude, obnoxious and tried to break up the inside of our ambulance!

One such case was for a man that gotten radiator fluid in his eyes. When we pulled up on scene, I could hear this guy yelling and screaming, and as Mike grabbed the jump bag, I retrieved the stretcher and went over to see what was going on. As I approached, I saw a medium-sized man that looked like a biker holding onto his head screaming, "I can't see." There was a hose running cold water from their house, so I picked it up and tried to run some water over his eyes, but the fool wouldn't close his mouth and kept choking on the water. He was extremely anxious and Mike tried to calm him down, but it was no use. So we walked him over to the ambulance and placed him on the stretcher. While en route to the hospital, the man became more and more worked up, and violent until finally I had to stop the ambulance and jump into the back to help Mike put him into four-point restraints.

And so the evening went. Mike would look at me and say, "I don't believe this! When you're in the back, you quietly do your paperwork and discuss fly fishing in Idaho, then when I'm in the back, I get every raving banshee on the planet! I'd say, "Awe Mike, it's just your personality. You have to be more kind and understanding." Mike would just shake his head.

8 AM Sunday 15 July, 1984

Morning arrived and Mike and I headed back to Station 1. All in all, it had been a fairly decent shift. Mike and I enjoyed each other's company and worked well together. Sort of funny, I had dreaded working with Mike at the start of the shift. I had heard so many reports about how Mike was hard to work with. Funny how I had no problems with him.

I hopped into my car and headed home. I grabbed my brown American Ambulance uniform, and was back to work by 8:30 AM. Robin Nunn and I were working together again today. We put our ambulance in order and on time. Fortunately, it was in pretty good shape. We began our day with the normal barrage of non-emergent calls to Desert Springs hospital and Rose de Lima hospital. The afternoon picked up with several emergent calls to include a cardiac arrest at the Riviera Casino.

The call involved a gentleman that had suddenly gone into cardiac arrest while playing slot machines, and collapsed in front of his machine. The Clark County Fire Department EMTs were doing CPR when we arrived. Robin cut open his shirt sleeve to look for a vein to start an IV and I grabbed the laryngoscope blade to intubate the patient. As I was visualizing his vocal cords, I heard the tell-tale gurgling sound of a patient getting ready to vomit. I shoved the ET tube down the esophagus and turned the tube to the side to prevent him from aspirating (vomiting into his lungs) or throwing up on me.

Oops! I turned the tube the wrong way and the vomit spewed out the tube and all over Robin's head and hair! As she was looking at me in shock and dismay, an elderly lady at the end of the row of slot machines grabbed her husband's arm and started walking towards us saying, "Oh look Harold, their filming a movie!"

For a moment, everyone stopped the resuscitation effort and looked at the elderly couple in dismay as well. If it weren't such a tragic mess, it would have been funny as hell!

The team quickly regained their composure and continued the resuscitation. I couldn't stop apologizing to Robin and once we turned the patient over to the Desert Springs ER staff, we quickly returned to the substation so that Robin could take a shower!

I'd been doing nothing but work lately and it was really starting to show. Nothing but work and sleep. Work and (some) sleep. And when I was sleeping, I was on call for work! I needed to get away. Time had slipped away by running call, after call, after call. The days and shifts began to run together with nothing unusual or different happening. All the heart attacks seem to be the same, and even though no two calls are supposed to be alike, they all seemed the same in the end. It was time for a change.

It was time for a party! My roommate Jim and I decided that next Saturday will be Las Vegas's first annual "Paramedic Burnout Party!"

The invitations were sent out, and the beer was brought in.

With the party as a goal, the rest of the week went by a little faster and easier. Everyone was invited, and everyone was excited to come. The party was at our house on 321 Xavier street, and began at 6:30 PM; pool, Jacuzzi, munchies, beer, and B. Y. O. B.! Be there aloha!

8 AM Saturday, 21 July, 1984

Party day. I am excited. The house is ready. My dad (Richard Flewelling) drove in from Chino, California for the event. Everyone is coming! Doctors and nurses from three hospitals; Firemen and paramedics from the Las Vegas and Clark County Fire Departments; Police officers from the Las Vegas Metro and Clark County Sheriff's Department, and even a couple Nevada Highway Patrol officers!

This party was going to be epic! My roommate, Jim bought all the food. At 6:30 PM, people started to show up. By 7:30 PM, the party was well underway and everyone was having a crazy time. At 8 PM it started raining, but that just made the party even wilder. People were being thrown into the pool, large amounts of beer were being consumed, and romance was everywhere. I have no idea how many people were there, but it was a sizable number. There were people everywhere; In the front yard, in the family room and kitchen. By the pool and in the bedrooms! I couldn't have gone to sleep even if I wanted too. At 11PM, the neighbors started to complain. The police stopped by twice with two requests, 1) we turn down the music , and 2) we keep the party going until they could get off shift!! By 2:30 AM, the party started slowing down, and by 5 AM only a few hard-core partiers were left. All of the food was gone. The two - 16 gallon kegs of beer had been emptied, and four large trash cans full of wine, beer and liquor bottles were all that remained of an extraordinary night. Over the course of the evening, so many people had been thrown into the pool, that I had given out all my scrub shirts, T-shirts and shorts to cold and shivering (mostly female) partiers. I hoped they remembered to return them!

At 6AM, I put clean sheets on my bed (for reasons I won't mention) and crawled in to take a nap. Jim was passed out in his room with about four other people, and my Dad was asleep on the couch. It was a fun event, but I was exhausted!

Noon Sunday, 22 July, 1984

I was surprised! It only took an hour or so to clean up the mess. It started raining hard, so the patio was naturally rinsed off. The pool and Jacuzzi were in decent shape. The water was dirty, due to all the beer that was dumped into them, but at least there were no bodies floating! The party had been an excellent stress reliever for everyone. I know it helped me to unwind. I got pretty crazy and slightly out of control at times, but I think people felt free enough to really release and let loose. There were a few arguments and a ton of venting, but all in all, everyone was well behaved. It provided me with a refreshed outlook on life and renewed energy to charge ahead into the future. I hoped it did the same for everyone else.

Shelly was there from start to finish of the party. I don't know where she slept, but when I woke up around noon, she was at my bed side telling me to get my lazy butt up.

I did what I was told and dressed in my last remaining scrub shirt and shorts. I had more than a modest hangover! By late afternoon, Shelley said, "You still look miserable. Lay down here on the living room floor and let me massage your back and neck." Not being one to turn down a free back massage, I found a pillow for my head and laid on the floor while Shelly massaged my back. It felt really good and was definitely diminishing my headache.

While Shelly massaged, I began to feel a light tickle under my shorts along the crease of my buttocks. I said, "Shelly, what are you doing?" With both her hands on my shoulders, she said, "I'm giving you a massage, you idiot." I said, "If both of your hands are massaging my back, whose is tickling my butt?!" As I stood up, a large water bug crawled out from under my shorts. Shelly replied, "Don't look as me. He's not mine!" I looked back at her skeptically and said, "Trained water bugs? Really, Shelly?" We both busted a gut laughing. From then on it was our secret joke. "Shelly Windholtz and her trained water bugs...."

Saturday, July 21 had been the start of four days off. I didn't have to go back to work until Tuesday, July 24. Monday was spent taking party supplies and kegs back to the supplier, straightening up the house. I draining the pool so that I could fill it with water rather than beer! I decided it was time to sit down and revamp the lecture I was giving on driving under the influence, which I was delivering to local Las Vegas high school students. Brilliant timing don't you think?

I formulated an updated plan and then set out to collect information. I went to the local police station to collect information, but learned that they didn't keep the statistics there. They suggested talking to the Highway Patrol. I went to the main Highway Patrol station, but they didn't have any information either. They did, however, have a telephone number for me. I called the number, and they advised that they (the Nevada Traffic Safety Commission) would love to help. I was on my way!

I had done these lectures before, but I wanted updated information. I wanted my lectures to be more effective, more compelling for young adults to be careful. Last year, I only spoke to students. This year I wanted to talk to their parents as well. I thought it would go over well. The county health office also helped me by rounding up films and literature to pass out to students and parents.

I also spent time talking to Dennis Nolan about what I intended to do. Dennis is an extraordinary young man who was only 22 years old. He had formed his own volunteer ambulance group and was contracted to do many of the special events around town. He had a large volunteer staff, taught emergency medical technician classes and had his own building. I was very grateful when he said he'd love to help me. Dennis had experience doing similar lectures in the past, was a native of Las Vegas and knew what did and didn't work.

I had gotten a lot of things done today and was quite pleased. Tonight I was going to watch the Las Vegas Stars play. The Las Vegas Stars are a minor-league baseball team for the San Diego

Padres. I was able to get into the games for free and received free sodas, simply by volunteering at their first aid booth.

There was quite a crowd starting to gather in the stadium, and talk about lots of pissed off fans when they found out that the game had been canceled due to the field being too wet from all the rain! Oh well, I made it through the short evening without a single patient, but I was also a bit disappointed about not getting to watch the game.

Tuesday, July 24, 1984

I'm back at work full of energy and ready to save lives! Well, I'm back to work anyway.

Today, I'm working with Paul Young, a 10-year veteran from the old American Ambulance company days. Paul worked for American Ambulance before American was purchased by Mercy Ambulance in 1982. I like working with Paul, he has a good sense of humor, was a straightforward paramedic and renders good patient care. He is also finishing Pre-Med courses at the University of Las Vegas. Paul has a hard time working with just anybody and was really glad to see me this morning, which was his first shift since returning from vacation.

Paul and I swiftly checked out the ambulance and went through the usual problems of trying to replace missing items that the off-going crew forgot. By 9:45 AM we were on the road. We received our first call just as we left the station, but were quickly canceled. We shut down our siren and turned off the lights just in time to catch the right exit to get food. We were a little early for lunch, so we grabbed a newspaper and went into the Desert Springs hospital cafeteria and relaxed until they opened up. The morning was quiet and relaxing. After we ate, we drove over to our substation only to realize that the departing crew had not left us the station keys! Totally pissed, we drove back to the main substation to retrieve them.

The afternoon was fairly busy for about six hours. We had about 20 minutes or less between calls. Then at around 6 PM we received a call that I will long remember. Paul and I were in the ambulance, and had just cleared from So. Ma. Mo. Hospital and were heading back to our area, when an anxious dispatcher came on the air and said "Medic two standby for code 3 dispatch." I looked over at Paul and said, "Must be something good, they sound pretty excited." Since I was driving, Paul grabbed the microphone with notepad in hand and said, "Medic two, go ahead." The dispatcher gave the call, "Medic two, 421, possible drowned child at district 2819 Phantom 34, at 5206 Post Ln. Respond code 3 with Rescue 22." Paul said, "10-4 medic two responding." I said "Talk about lucky, Rescue 22 has just become a paramedic substation and they are a lot closer than we are." I turned on the lights and sirens, and accelerated onto Interstate 15. I said, "I'll get off on Tropicana Blvd., Paul you'll have to lead me in from there." Paul was feverishly looking through the map book trying to find the best route. Once deciphered, Paul said, "head west on Tropicana to Decatur and then head south. This is on a gravel road. I hope we can get through." I followed Paul's instructions and headed west on Tropicana and to our horror saw Rescue 22 heading east! I said, "Paul what's going on here?" Paul got back on the radio and advised dispatch that Rescue 22 was running code 3 East on Tropicana at Wynn Road, and to check with Fire Department dispatch as to which ambulance was heading the right direction.

We continued on the route Paul had given me. We arrived on scene 15 minutes ahead of Rescue 22. The father of the child and a family friend were doing CPR on a 16 month old girl that was found in the family pool by her father. Paul and I immediately went into action. I intubated the child and started her on one hundred percent oxygen, ventilating with an ambu bag. Paul placed the ECG monitor on her and then tried to start an IV line. The father was still doing chest compressions and was starting to emotionally break down, so we had him leave the room. By this time the Fire Department had arrived and took over chest compressions. Several attempts were made to start an IV, but the veins were so small and the child too cold. It was impossible to get a line started. Our ECG monitor was showing complexes at a rate of 10 bpm, with no pulse. Chest compressions continued with good pulses felt. Since we had complexes, we needed to speed up the heart rate, so 0.5 mg of epinephrine was given down the endotracheal tube. No initial results were noted. People started showing up from everywhere, so we decided to move the resuscitation efforts into the ambulance where we could control the scene better. Once in the ambulance, we managed to get an IV started and pushed half an amp of sodium bicarb to correct acidosis. The girls skin color, which had initially been quite gray and cyanotic was now more pink. Suddenly the little girl's heart rate increased from 10 to 80 bpm and a spontaneous pulse was felt. Her blood pressure was low at first, but increased by the time we reached the emergency room.

While still on scene, the family physician arrived and rode into the hospital with us. I'm sure she'll never forget the experience. I'll never forget it. Just before we were about ready to leave, a priest jumped into the side door and started to bless the little girl. This would have been all right except he was getting in the way and Paul couldn't ventilate the child. Paul looked up at him and said, "Don't you think you're jumping the gun a little bit padre?" The priest said, "I think it's already too late." Paul turned red in the face and said, "It ain't over until I say it's over! Now get out of my ambulance, now!!!" With that, the priest left. Paul looked up at me in the front and said, "What fucking nerve!"

I shook my head and pulled away from the scene. The drive back was a difficult one. I had to be extra careful since there were people working in the back of my ambulance that were not used to being there, and between people yelling at me to "speed up" and "slow down", "stop" and "go", "turn the siren off" and "turn the siren on", "answer the radio" and "what did the ER say?" We finally made it! Once in the emergency room, another IV was started and the little girl was making respiratory effort on her own. The family physician was happy. The ER doc was happy, and we, the paramedics were elated! It was a good feeling to know that through all our training and hours in the fields, we can actually produce miracles once in a while!

After the call, came the fun job of restocking the ambulance. We used just about everything! The ambulance was a total mess and took over an hour to restock. The rest of the shift felt pretty anti-climactic.

Both Paul and I were famished, so we grabbed a quick bite to eat while we were still at Sunrise hospital and then headed back to our substation for some rest. Once in the substation, I sacked out on my bed and started thinking about how lucky that little girl was. If Paul and I had turned around and followed Rescue 22, she would have been dead by now. I also thought back to the little boy that Robin and I had been too late for, and I wished we would have had the same opportunity as we had today. It's tough when you live in "ultra-reality." One has to learn to accept the things you can't change, and do your best to change the things you can. Paul and I were up and down with calls most of the evening. None of the patients were all that serious; a laceration here, chest pain there, a fainting episode, so on and so forth. Just enough business to keep us up and tired by the end of the shift.

I don't know what it is, but watching the sun come up after working the night through makes me even more tired. Sort of the last sign that says, "Yep, you were up all night long." The end of the shift couldn't come soon enough.

8:30 AM Wednesday, 25 July, 1984

Paul and I cleaned the ambulance and turned it over to the on-coming crew. Funny how they never have as much problem cleaning the ambulance and being ready to start as we do.

As I walked by the office at Station 1, Carmen (one of the Mercy Admin girls) called to me and said that she had a couple of things for me. It was the literature from the traffic and safety commission in Carson City. It had arrived and there was a note to call a woman at the Metro police station about a possible child abuse case. The call was in reference to a case I was very familiar with; it involving the six-year-old boy that we were too late to resuscitate. I called Robin and told her. She felt the same way I did "sick." This job never cuts you any slack.

I found an empty office and worked for a couple hours with the new lecture material I had just received. Just as I was about to walk out the door, a dispatcher cornered me and begged me to work half the shift today (12 hours). I said, "If you can't find anyone else, I will cover, but you have got to make an honest effort to find someone."

As soon as I arrived home the phone rang, "Can you come in at 8 o'clock tonight?" With a heavy sigh I said, "I'll be there." Knowing that I had to work a 24 hour shift tomorrow, and realizing that I had just set myself up for a 36-hour shift, I went to bed and unplugged the phone.

My alarm clock went off at 6:30 PM and I got ready for work. I am working the 12 hour the shift with Serge Levy. Serge has a very unusual background; born in Morocco, raised in Israel, joined the U.S. military as a Marine, and worked for various ambulance services across the United States. All that being said, he's a Zionistic Israeli Jew through and through! Something that I deeply admired. He displayed a passion and a belief that was unshakable.

That being said, his life experiences and religious beliefs gave him a very twisted view on life. He is a real nice person to be around off-duty and around the substation, but as far as his medical skills are concerned, I have to rate him as average. Serge had a problem handling non-life threatening calls. I think he felt that they are a waste of his time or something. His care for non-emergent patients was pretty lousy. Unfortunately for Serge, non—life threatening calls represent a larger percentage of our call volume, which made Serge a difficult person to work with. But as always, I tried to get along with everyone.

The shift was fairly mild, with only six calls and four transports. Unfortunately for Serge, none were life-threatening.

Serge and I had a late call in the morning, which made me have to hustle to get from the North Las Vegas substation to Station 1 to begin my 24 hour shift on American Ambulance.

8:50 AM Thursday, 26 July, 1984

I'm working with Paul Young today. The morning had its usual amount of confusion and false starts, but we managed to get away by 9:30 AM. Once away from the main station, things slowed down. We were able to get breakfast and drove to our substation. Fortunately, I was able to sleep most of the morning. The afternoon became "airport day." It seemed like people were constantly getting sick or falling down from one end of the airport to the other. The American Ambulance substation is the closest ambulance substation to the airport and therefore routinely the first Unit called for airport emergencies. McCarran International airport had just changed their gate numbers, which caused quite a bit of confusion getting to the proper location. While Paul and I had airport badges to enter the airport grounds, but we had to be escorted by a vehicle in communication with the ground control tower. Even those guys were getting confused today!

27, 28, 29, 30, 31 July, 1984

The hours ran on and the calls kept coming in. Those hours turned into days and days into a week. I've been working so much lately that fatigue made remembering calls difficult. Friday, July 27, I was off but got called back in due to rain and tons of accidents. Saturday, July 28, I worked a 24-hour shift. Sunday, July 29, I worked a 24-hour shift. Monday, July 30 I worked a 16-hour shift, and Tuesday, July 31 I worked a 12-hour shift.

By Tuesday, I was burnt out, I could barely remember what ambulance I was working, let alone what kind of calls I went on. The numbness between my eye was a permanent fixture. My whole head was starting to feel numb. I was just going through the motions on impulse mode.

I was so tired and grumpy, I think everyone was glad that I went home and got some sleep!

I had gone to work on Wednesday morning, July 25 and was now going home at 8 PM Tuesday, July 31! I don't even remember undressing. All I know is that I did not wake up until Wednesday afternoon August 1.

3 - SUPERVISORS AND GROIDS

1 PM Wednesday, 1 August, 1984

I awoke and showered. Feeling good, I drove down to the Mercy Ambulance, Station 1 to make a few long-distance phone calls. I needed to track down additional teaching material for my drinking and driving lecture. My goal was to use high quality, up-to-date information to improve the impact and relevance of the presentation.

The girls in the business office were teasing me about being in there so much that they were going to give me an office day and the desk. Some days, I'd have to agree!

Settling into my "day office", I began making calls. One of my calls was to the U.S. Department of Transportation, Materials Center, Highway Safety Research Institute, in Ann Arbor, MI. I got a chuckle out of the woman I spoke to on the phone. I asked her if she could send me recent data on traffic safety statistics, as well as any info on the topic of drunk driving and alcohol countermeasures. She cheerfully said, "I'll be glad to send you everything we have! In fact, if you pay my way, I'll deliver it to you in person!" I laughed and said, "Sorry, I'm on a fixed budget."

The rest of the day was spent running little errands here and there. I returned home at 5:30 PM, cleaned my pool and laid around the house for the rest of the evening. It was during down times like this that I became slightly depressed about my lack of a social life, but I just didn't have the time to invest; not that I hadn't tried a couple of times since I arrived to Las Vegas, but nothing had ever worked out. I know most of it had to do with my insane work hours. Oh well, I wasn't worried. I'd have more time in the future. Maybe, until then, there are girls out there that only wanted to date on a casual basis. It was once put to me, "the swath is too wide and too deep to worry about any single one." I thought there was some truth in that.

My roommate, Jim, had been disappointing me lately. His last rent check bounced, and everyone but Jim has told me that he's moving out. This is a distraction that I just didn't need, not to mention the financial burden. Well, things had always worked out in the past and I was sure they would again. It is 11 PM and I thought I'd go to bed a little early tonight.

While lying in bed, when it's quiet and nobody else is around, crazy thoughts run through your mind. I think about things I've done in the past back in Iowa, the guys at the Woodbury County Sheriff's Department; I wonder how many will move on, or change to a different line of work. I wonder if I'm unique in having to keep the ball constantly rolling. Man, some of those guys back there could really do good in places like Los Angeles, Las Vegas, or Denver. If only they knew or even had the ambition to know, and the courage to find out.

I wondered how my new lecture would turn out, how many groups would I engage, and whether it would even be effective. One could only hope. There were still so many variables in my life, some days I thought my goals were so clear cut and precise, and then other days I was hardly sure if I was heading in the right direction. No sense worrying, it was time to sleep.

8 AM Thursday, 2 August, 1984

I arrived to work and was thrilled to learn that I would be working with Paul Young again. I was supposed to work with Nancy Martin, since Robin Nunn was still out with a back injury. I had arrived to work a little early, and went to the supply store to grab the typical items needed to restock the ambulance. My efforts allowed us to restock the ambulance the moment it arrived at the station. Paul and I were able to get out of Station 1 in minutes. We spent most of the day in the ambulance, but not much time on calls. Paul had a few errands to run and so did I, so we just buzzed from one place to another. The calls were few and none were life-threatening; just enough to say we earned our paycheck. As I recall, we had a syncopal episode (fainting) at the airport, in which a few lovely stewardesses were kind enough to give us assistance; a possible heart attack that appeared stable; a little old man that couldn't remember if he took his medicine, but ended up taking it three times (we received this call as an overdose); Ah yes, and the actor/entertainer, Mr. Robert Goulet himself!

Mr. Goulet was an extremely nice gentleman. He had what we call, a primary seizure (a first-time seizure) prior to our arrival. Initially, Mr. Goulet was really out of it. He was semi-conscious when we placed him into the ambulance. I was the attendant and started to work on him. I placed him on oxygen and started an IV; At this time he started to come around. He opened his eyes and looked around the inside of the ambulance. When he noticed me, he calmly said, "Hello." I said, "Hi." He politely asked "Where am I?" I said, "Well sir, you are in the back of my ambulance. It kind of looks like you had a seizure." "A seizure!" he said, "That is kind of bad isn't it?" I said, "Well, it can be." Mr. Goulet and I carried on a nice conversation en route to the hospital. He was now fully awake and had no complaints or discomforts. I reassessed him and could find no injuries or neurological deficits. Once at the hospital, I finished my medical reports and took a moment to speak with Mr. Goulet's wife, Vera. She was also a very pleasant and gracious woman. I explained what probably happened and told her that he was going to be all right. We sat and chatted for a little while and before I left she gave me her card and told me to give them a call whenever I wanted to see one of Robert's shows. A gracious offer, but completely unnecessary.

Paul and I cleaned the ambulance and headed back over to our substation. The rest of the day was pretty relaxing, only a few calls and many were non-transports. One of Paul's girlfriends came over to visit and brought her roommates' little girl with her, who was an absolute doll. While Paul was off talking to Barbara, I kept Atara happy. We played little games my grandparents used to play with me when I was little, like "the little spider up the leg" or "this little piggy went to the market with her toes." She was a happy, bubbly little girl and a joy to be around. When Barbara and Atara left, Paul and I tried to get some sleep. We had no sooner fallen asleep when we received a call for a patient in distress 25 miles out of Las Vegas. The call was for a woman having chest pain.

A new term had popped up amongst paramedics in Las Vegas. The term was called "ghost busting", which meant taking care of illnesses that weren't really there. This girl was such a spook. She was no sicker than I was. She had been pulled over for a speeding ticket and was trying to get out of it. No such luck. No transports for her. We went back to bed, but were again quickly roused to respond to another ill woman.

This time, the woman really was sick. She was showing all the symptoms of a major stroke. While her illness was legitimate, she had one of those "Julia Child" voices that were like fingernails on a chalk board! As you can tell, my bedside manner dropped considerably at 5 AM, but I did manage to keep my composure and render appropriate care. As we left the hospital, the sun was coming up; and you know that is the one thing that I can't stand, watching the sun come up at work. I was fine with calls that came before the sun came up or calls that happened after the sun came up, I just didn't want to be on a call as the sun came up.

8:30 AM Friday, 3 August, 1984

I drove to the Clark County Community College to listen to a lecture on the paramedic national registry test that I was going to take on the 13th of August. The lecture had started at 8 AM, so I was a bit late. As I walked in, everyone was taking an old national registry exam to get a feel for what the exam would be like. Since I was late, everyone had to wait for me to finish my practice exam. I think I could've done a better job, but being rushed and tired, I was only able to pull off an 82% (70% is passing). I managed to stay awake while a couple guys talked about the testing procedures. Noon couldn't come soon enough!

At noon I drove home, change clothes and made myself some lunch before heading over to help Paul's girlfriend, Jill move to a new appartment. It was misery. She was moving from one upstairs apartment to another upstairs apartment. The temperature was over 100° and both Paul and I were dead tired. Paul had initially promised that it would be only a couple hours' work. Well, at 5 PM I was finally dragging my tired bones home. I laid down on my bed and thought, "I'll just lay here for a couple hours." At 11 PM, six hours later, I woke up and thought, "well shoot there goes another day." I got up anyway and worked on my drinking and driving program lecture. That old typewriter the folks gave me many moons ago had really typed its money's worth. At 2:30 AM I finally went back to bed. I had to be back at work at 8 AM that morning.

8 AM Saturday, 4 August, 1984

Incredibly, I wasn't tired as I arrived to work. I was working with Mike Sherwood today out of Substation 9 (The supervisor's substation). I started checking out the ambulance and was very disappointed to find it in the same poor shape as any other ambulance. I could understand being busy, but to leave an ambulance without oxygen or IV solutions was uncalled for, and especially in a supervisor's ambulance; but I stocked it up to par and put the ambulance in service with dispatch. Mike and I had a "third rider" shadowing us today. Third riders can be guests riding on the ambulance to see if it's a profession they would like to enter, or other medical professionals gaining pre-hospital care experience. Our rider's name was Jennifer Painter, a fellow paramedic riding along so that she could study with Mike for the national registry exam in between calls.

Our first call of the day was an automobile accident on Interstate 15 at the Sahara off-ramp. Mike, Jennifer and I responded. As we approached the Sahara off-ramp, we noticed Nevada Highway Patrol stopped in the opposite direction at the scene of an automobile accident. We skipped through the median and stopped to see if this was the accident we were called to. It wasn't, so we turned around and proceeded through the medium again to find the right accident. We didn't get very far. (At this point I must say that I was *not* driving!). Mike went into the median straight-on instead of approaching it at an angle, and high-centered the ambulance. He put it into reverse but the ambulance just spun it's tires and didn't move an inch. He tried going forward but the results were the same.

I looked out my side windows and saw that the back tires were dug in about 5 inches and I knew that there was no hope. I got on the radio and said, "Dispatch, this Unit is 10-7, stuck in the median. Can you send another ambulance to the 401." Dispatch replied "10-4" (Understood).

Mike had stepped out of the ambulance and came running back to the cabin saying, "You didn't tell them we were stuck did you?" I said in a matter of fact manner, "Yes I did. I told them to send another ambulance to the 401." Mike retorted, "We are not stuck!

I'm going to try one more thing. We are not stuck I tell you!" I said, "Mike, we're stuck." Mike replied, "How do you know?" I said, "For the love-of-Pete Mike, I looked!" There was no hope in calming Mike down. He knew he had been caught with his pants down and there was nothing he could do about it. He tried to chew me out for getting on the radio and saying we were stuck. As we watched the second ambulance responding to the accident drive by (pointing and laughing at us) Mike said, "You see how long it took for those guys to get here? We could have been out and there by now." I said, "SURE! IF we could have gotten loose, we could have just canceled the other crew and handled it ourselves, but if you haven't noticed Mike, we're still STUCK and they're on scene! Which is another good reason for calling in immediately upon getting stuck. Since it took so long for them to get there, there is no need to delay a response any longer than possible with us messing around for 10 minutes trying to determine if we are just stuck or really, REALLY stuck!

"Face it, Mike, you messed up! It happens to everyone, you're no different than me!" Mike just grumbled for a little while, then he came up with a new argument. "Well, you used improper radio procedure! You should have called them on the phone or just said that we were 10 - 7. You didn't have to let the whole world know we were stuck!" I chuckled and said, "All right Mike, you got me there. I didn't use proper radio procedure." LVFD Rescue 4 was returning to their station from the accident that we never made it to, and we managed to wave them down to ask if they had a chain that could pull us out. They did and we were finally free from the median.

Mike was trying so hard to maintain his "supervisor image," but to no avail. I wouldn't let up. If he would have just admitted to the fact that he messed up, I would have dropped the topic in a heartbeat, but he wouldn't admit any fault and I was relentless. "Awe come on Mike, cheer up. I forgive you. Frank, (Mercy ambulance's senior mechanic) is going to blow a gasket when he finds out, but I forgive you. By the way, how much are you going to pay me to keep my mouth shut?" Mike would spit and sputter, but he knew there was nothing he could do and I was loving every minute.

The next few calls were routine nursing home calls, an infant with an elevated temp that had experienced a febrile seizure, and a couple of canceled calls.

We dropped Jennifer off at her car and continued work. The next call of significance was at the Meadows Mall. I said to Mike, "Probably an elderly person attacked by an escalator!" Escalators may be great "people movers", but if you have limited mobility and an unstable gait, those things become monsters with teeth. I remembered one particular elderly gentleman that told me he tried to fight it off but it was too strong and had relentlessly kept "biting" him. "If it wasn't for somebody pulling me away, it probably would have eaten me alive!"

At the mall, we found an elderly Iranian man that was witnessed falling to the ground clutching his chest. The gentleman was awake as we approached him, but he spoke no English. Unlike Spanish, where I can pretty much get the general drift of what is being said, I couldn't understand anything this man was trying to say. While there was no one around him, he kept looking for someone, which left us to believe there was a family member or friend in the mall that he knew and could perhaps interpret for us.

The man was short of breath, extremely sweaty and pale, and was clutching his chest. While security looked for an interpreter, I managed to get my monitor hooked up to him and put him on oxygen. My ECG monitor confirmed what I suspected, he had a wide QRS complex, a P-R interval of over .20, and elevated S-T segment with an extremely high T wave, which indicated an acute cardiac condition. In layman's terms, if he didn't receive immediate treatment he would be a dead man by morning.

He was quite anxious (with good reason) sitting in a chair and starting to wobble a little. So I told the firefighters to bring the ambulance gurney over and that we would put him on it while we waited for an interpreter. I tried to explain what I wanted him to do, but was failing miserably. I finally just picked up the man and sat him on the ambulance stretcher. I thought to myself, "Well, he let me put him on oxygen and hook him up to the monitor. I wonder if he will let me start an IV?" No such luck. His sweating increased and the monitor began to show premature ventricular contractions. He then pulled out a medicine bottle and swallowed another capsule. I asked him if I could see the bottle. There wasn't any label on the bottle, the pills were green & yellow capsules that looked like 500 mg Inderal tablets, a big gun cardiac medication. One of the firefighters approached to relate that he had already taken one of these pills earlier upon their arrival (five minutes earlier). I turned to the man and tried to ask him how many he had taken. The man took the open pill bottle, pointed inside the bottle saying something foreign, and then took another capsule. I was in shock. "Spit it out!" I urged. I shook my head and said "no, no!" Now, on top of his heart problems, which I was unsure of, I knew definitely he had overdosed on his medication, whatever it was.

The mall security guards came through for us, and found a family member of the man in question. I said "Thank God!" "Sir, ask him how many capsules he has taken." The family member, a middle-aged Iranian man, asked "What's going on here?" I said, "Your friend is having a heart attack. Ask how much of his medicines he has taken." The man said, "He's not having a heart attack, he's always short of breath, he takes his medicine and is all better." I said, "Sir, he is having major heart problems today and would you please ask him how much medication he has taken. The family member asked the elderly man the question in a foreign language, who opened the bottle held up one finger, then took another capsule. I screamed "no!" The family member said, "He said he has only taken one." I said, "That is not true, I've seen him take 4 capsules since we've been here." I asked the family interpreter to ask him which hospital he would like to go to, but the family member said he did not want to go to the hospital. By this time my nerves were shot. "Sir", I said, "He has got to go to the hospital. There is a good chance he could die if he doesn't." The family member said, "He was just in the doctor's office the other day and was fine. Why isn't he fine now?" I said, "Sir, heart problems can come on very fast, he needs to go to the hospital." The family member said, "Oh, he will be fine, he has these spells all the time." I said, "Sir, this is my job. I specialize in medical emergencies and what I see is a man that, unless he receives immediate attention, will most likely die." I implored, would you please convince him to go in and get checked out. If he won't go with us, will you at least take him in yourself?"

The elderly man's relative became increasingly arrogant and refused to cooperate. They asked the elderly man if he wanted to go to the hospital, which they reported he did not, but they wouldn't try to insist that he go. They wouldn't tell him that we thought there was a good chance that he would die if he didn't seek urgent medical care. Completely flustered, we had him sign a card stating that we (the paramedics) thought it imperative that he seek medical attention, and that he refused to go. After the form was signed, I turned to the mall security guards and said, "He refuses to go with us. We are going to leave. I suggest that you escort them off the property, because there is a good chance he may collapse on you very soon." The security guards said, "okay." Mike and I packed up our equipment and headed out the door. "Can you believe how ignorant people can be?" I said to Mike. "That person will probably be dead in the morning, and that family is going to wonder why." "No wonder Iran is a messed up country! With intelligence like that, it's going to stay that way for a long time!"

Once in the ambulance, we notified dispatch we were cleared from the call. I said, "Mike, I think that's one of the toughest things to deal with. Knowing there is much that can be done and not being able or allowed to do it." Mike replied, "I know, but there's nothing we can do."

The next few calls fell into the realm of "Groid" calls; that is to say self-inflicted medical problems like malnutrition, acute intoxication, and poor hygiene habits.

The "Groids" continued on through the night, while Mike's attitude didn't improve. Everyone had heard about Mike getting the ambulance stuck in the median and were reminding him of it all night long. But he still wouldn't fess up to the fact that it was his fault!

First, it was my fault, because I pointed out the wrong accident. How was I to know that there were three accidents within ½ mile of each other? Then it was my fault because I didn't clear him on my side of the ambulance. I just said, "Mike, you didn't even make it to the highway to get cleared!"

As long as Mike was in denial, I continued to goad him. I'd say "Mike, I sure like working with you. I mean it is so educational and exciting." Mike would say, "What you mean?" I'd say, "Well, the last time we worked together, you kept getting beat up by the patients. Today, the Iranian was a real challenge and I even learned how not to drive through medians; and I'm inspired by your mastery of the long-lost art of passing the buck!" Mike would say, "What do you mean passing the buck?" I'd just say "Think about it." Mike clammed up and stared straight ahead as we drove on in silence.

Our next call was for possible seizure that turned out to be a man with a very low blood sugar. Mike and I joined the Fire Department paramedics in stabilizing this patient. We placed him on oxygen and started an IV. While Mike was administering an ampoule of dextrose, out of the blue he said "You think I'm blaming you for what happened earlier today don't you." I stopped what I was doing and looked at Mike in total amazement. I said, "It's a vicious rumor Mike, just a vicious rumor." Sometimes I wonder about him... On second thought, I wondered about Mike all the time. How he became a shift supervisor I'll never know.

The evening turned into morning and we were still running calls. I was so tired that I didn't even harass Mike. As the hours stretched on, the calls began to blend together; the blood pressures all sounded the same, as did the patient's past medical history. You could almost walk up to a heart patient and say, let me guess, you are on nitroglycerin, Lasix, Inderal, and quinidine. You saw your doctor last week and he said you were okay. You started experiencing chest pain half an hour before calling us." The patient would most likely come back with, "Well, ... I waited an hour before calling."

Once again, I watched the sun come up to the sound of my siren. I was so glad when 8 AM arrived and this shift came to an end. As Mike and I cleaned up the ambulance, I couldn't help myself. I said, "Well Mike, what have we learned in the last 24 hours?" Mike just said, "Go away!" I laughed as I headed for the office, "Mike, as I say to all the paramedics I work with at the end of the shift – it's been a real inconvenience."

8 AM Sunday, 5 August, 1984

Fellow Mercy Ambulance paramedic, Ron Barnes, was the guy that had helped me get hired as a paramedic in Las Vegas. Ron and I had attended paramedic school together in Iowa and had worked together on two ambulance services in Sioux City. Ron left Iowa for Las Vegas about nine months before I did and had encouraged me and others in Sioux City to apply for work at Mercy.

Ron was also just getting off work. As we greeted each other he said, "I just ran the strangest call I've had in a while. We responded to the airport for a 'man down' that turned out to be a dead Iranian guy that family members were trying to fly back to Iran! They thought that since he had a ticket that would just plop him into his plane seat and take him home! Could you imagine getting the seat next to him??"

Needless to the say the airlines wasn't having any of that!" I told Ron that I had probably ran on the very same guy and told the family during that call that he was a dead man walking!

Ron and his wife Pat, and their new son, Travis were going to Huntington Beach, CA for his two days off. I had the same two days off, so Ron asked if I wanted to come along. I said sure! I went home and changed clothes and fell asleep until Ron came to pick me up.

Ron was a few years older than I was and had really been there when I needed him. He helped me get the job in Las Vegas, and allowed me to stay at his place until I received my first paycheck and was able to get a place of my own. His wife Patricia (Pat) was equally as amazing. I'm pretty sure most wives would have grumbled if their husbands had said, "Hey Honey, an old colleague of mine is coming to live with us for a few weeks!" Pat was an extremely gracious host. I tried my best to make as small a foot print as possible in their tiny apartment and was diligent to move into my own place just as quickly as I could.

Ron and Pat had also recently had their "15 minutes of fame" during the birth of their son. Travis was their first and Ron had been at work when Pat went into labor. Being the dutiful husband, Ron called dispatch and related that he needed to go home to take his wife to the hospital. Dispatch had said not to worry, they would take him and his partner out of service so that they could pick her up and go to Desert Springs Hospital. This being Pat's first child, no one was in too much of a hurry. That is, until Pat's water broke and her contractions became less than a minute apart. Ron and his partner quickly placed Pat into the ambulance, but before they could even head for the hospital, it became clear that delivery was imminent. I don't think they even left the apartment compound parking lot. Ron delivered Travis right then and there! The Vegas news was all over the story! It made the local TV channels as well as the Associated

Press and the newspapers back in Iowa!

While I have delivered a dozen babies in my short paramedic career, I think I would be a basket case if I had to deliver my own!

Paramedic delivering own son is former city resident

An Associated Press story published in The Journal Wednesday reported that a Las Vegas, Nev. paramedic had delivered his first-born child en route to a hospital.

The paramedic, Ron Barnes, is a former resident of Sioux City. He is the son of Dakota County Assessor Betty Barnes O'Neill of South Sioux City and Lester Barnes of Sioux City.

Barnes received training as a paramedic in a program conducted by Western Iowa Tech Community College. He was employed by Midwest Ambulance in Sioux City before moving to Las Vegas last November.

Mrs. Barnes parents, Mr. and Mrs. Joseph Brogan, live at Sergeant Bluff.

Although "helping deliver babies is routine for paramedics," the Associated Press story stated, "Ron Barnes will always remember the fifth time he helped with a birth: The newborn was his own son.

"Barnes said he had planned to drive to the hospital when his wife, Patricia, who was nine days overdue, began having labor pains. The pains strengthened so quickly that he called Mercy Ambulance, his employer.

Travis Michael, the couple's first child, arrived midway through the ambulance ride, weighing 7 pounds, 6 ounces."

Mrs. O'Neill said Wednesday that at first she thought her son was kidding when he called and told her, "I just delivered you a nice baby grandson."

The Barnes family and I headed to Southern California at around 11 AM and pulled into the city of Huntington Beach at around 4 PM. After a day and a half of working, I was ready for some rest and relaxation. We were staying at Ron's aunt's home, who was very excited to see her new nephew. Once settled into the house, Ron and I headed for the beach. This was the first time this 'Iowa Boy' had ever gone swimming in the ocean, and let me tell you it was quite an experience!

I had a blast, but I think someone should do something about the taste! Too salty! Ron and I headed back to his aunt's house at around 8 PM. After eating supper, we all headed over to the Boones Farm area to see the sights until 11 PM, then we returned to the house and fell soundly asleep.

10 AM Monday, 6 August, 1984

I was all fired up to go to the beach for some "prime time girl watching!" The morning fog burned off around 11 AM and I was ready for the beach. Ron and Pat had people to visit so they dropped me off and said, "Have fun." I waived saying, "Pick me up around 5 PM tonight." The scenery was spectacular; and the ocean was pretty nice too. I tried my hand at surfing and a thing called a boogie board (California's answer to the snow saucer I used to ride down snowy hills back in Iowa) time flies when you're having fun and before I knew it, it was 5 PM and time to go back to Ron's aunt's place. I will definitely come back and visit again. I might just have to look into Santa Anna (a city in Southern California that Mercy is considering expanding service to.)

We arrived back into Las Vegas at midnight and I thanked Ron and Pat for taking me along. It was a wonderful spur of the moment get-away and I was extremely grateful. As Ron dropped me off, I reflected on going for months straight without a break, and felt the damage it had caused me now. I love what I do, but an excess of even a good thing is not a good thing.

6 AM Tuesday, 7 August 1984

Something I forgot to mention yesterday. Eight hours of fun in the sun doesn't occur without leaving its mark. I hurt! I am SOOO sunburnt from head to toe! Upon arriving to work, my partner Dan Windler, just laughed. "Serves you right! Going there and having a fun time without me!" Dan is a fantastic partner to work with; easy-going, mild-mannered, and a skilled paramedic. We were working Substation 5 today (The African-American side of town). Everyone was giving me a hard time this morning; "Ty, it looks like you got a little color over the weekend." I'd say, "Yah, about as much color as a ripe tomato!" The day drew on and none of the calls were very intense; an elderly women who slipped and fell at the mall, fracturing her ankle; a couple minor automobile accidents with patients complaining of neck and back pain; and of course the inevitable "Groids."

Dan and I seem to agree on just about everything we talked about. Dan would say, "I never knew that when I became a paramedic, part of my job description would be thief! I'd say, "it's not classified as thief, it's called 'appropriations and redistribution of hospital medical supplies'." I figured that a thief stole for his own personal gain, where we were acquiring medical supplies for the betterment of advanced emergency care. Dan would say, "Yeah that's what I said, thief!" I'd laugh and say, "I guess you're right, Thief."

The conversation bounced from topic to topic as we drove through our district looking for the most beautiful women we could find. We would cruise the Las Vegas strip, drive-by hotel pools, upscale malls, and supermarkets. Working from Mercy ambulance is not like the movie "Mother, Jugs and Speed." It's more like... "Moms, Falsies and Dexatrim!"

The evening was busy with back-to-back calls, but when you have a good partner you can handle anything. Dan and I were invincible. Every time we had a patient that was a total jerk, Dan and I would start into one of our acts. For example, one patient that was a "high roller" from Texas; I'd be in the back with the patient (the patient's real problem was typically insignificant, usually a headache or something stupid). I'd say, "What do ya think about faggots? The patient would answer in a southern drawl, "I cain't stand em, I think they should shoot 'em all." I'd yell up front where Dan is driving in a femmy voice, "Did you hear that Danny! Some people just have no respect for other people's lifestyles? I'd hold my head and say, "I can't handle this animosity! Daniel you sit back here with him; I don't want to." Dan would reply in a similar femmy voice, "No way! I don't want nothing to do with that, that MAN!" By this time, the patient doesn't know what to think and just looks at us in amazement.

Then there is the patient that calls for an ambulance and is standing on the street corner with a suitcase waving his social welfare card. We'd usually pull up just past him and continue driving slowly around the block just fast enough to keep the patient running behind the ambulance. Then finally stopping after two or three trips around the block, stepping out of the rig and say in a surprised voice, "Oh! Are you the one that called for an ambulance?" The "Groids" kept our funny bones tickled most of the evening. Some of the things we do to patients may sound mean, but then so many people have told me that the only reason they called us instead of a taxicab is because they had no money, and so all we are doing is giving them a glorified taxicab ride to the hospital. We figured, we might as well make it a memorable event!

30 August, 1984

Once again I am behind in my journal writing. Since you are now familiar with how I spent most of my time, I'll try to catch you up on news and events at Mercy.

Life has been fantastic. Work is going extremely well. They are finally putting me with a regular partner, at least the same half-dozen partners instead of floating me around like before. Mercy ambulance is thinking of going to 12 hour shifts instead of the 24 hour shifts we currently run, which would mean more money for less hours' work.

This would average out to about the same amount of money we are making now, but only working 80 hours instead of the 120 hours we currently work per pay period. Business also looks good for the Laughlin Nevada operations. Business is picking up and the crews are settling down. Santa Anna is also a hopeful prospect for the future. Lastly, my lectures on drunk driving are complete and I can't wait to introduce the new material.

Just as life was hitting the fast-track, set-back struck me. I have to retake a portion of my National Registry Paramedic practical exam. This is the first time I've ever failed a test and it was very hard to swallow. I went out into the mountains south of town to reflect on this failure. Several other paramedics at work failed the entire exam and went out drinking, or did drugs after being told they had failed. I on the other hand, took the high road and went out and beat up on some Joshua trees! But I'm okay now. So what if I'm not perfect anymore, I don't care....

I WAS FRAMED, THEY WERE ALL OUT TO GET ME!!!!!

I'm back. I went away for a little while, but I'm okay now.

All I have to do is go in and retake the one station that I missed and then I'll be registered. So it is not as bad as I made it out to be, it just hurt my pride.

I've had several very exciting calls recently. While I can't remember the times or dates, the details are still fresh in my mind. In one shift, I had several patients giving me the funniest excuses for calling an ambulance: One gentleman called an ambulance from a payphone downtown and said that he would meet us on the corner of fourth and Ogden Street. I thought to myself, "Oh boy, another "Groid" call!" We arrived to the street corner and this man came staggering up to the ambulance and said, "Take me to the hospital, I'm a sick human being!" I looked at him and kind of chuckled, and said "That you are Sir, that you are!" His major problem, was that he was an alcoholic who lived on the streets and was going into delirium tremens (DT's). We transported him to the Las Vegas Detox Center.

This gentleman was followed by another intoxicated soul that called an ambulance because, "He was sick and tired of being sick and tired." His only problem was that he was internally swimming in alcohol. We transported him to the detox center as well. My partner and I "hee hawed" about those two most of the evening.

I also treated several seriously injured patients. One morning, my partner (Nancy Martin) and I were going through the usual morning chaos when we received a call on the other (northside) of town, 20 minutes away, for a "man down."

We had been given the address of a Denny's restaurant in the area. When we arrived on scene we couldn't find Rescue. We thought that since it took such a long time for us to get on scene, that the patient must have refused treatment and they had already left. We called dispatch to check and was advised that Rescue was still on scene. I went into the restaurant and asked if they had called for an ambulance. They answered "No," but they would ask if anyone needed one. Talk about confidence in their cooking! I said, "Thanks, but that's not necessary." I went out to the ambulance to advise dispatch that no one had even called an ambulance at this address. Dispatch then gave us a new location - five blocks away from the restaurant, behind a Safeway grocery store in an abandoned house. When we arrived to that location we still couldn't find rescue and there wasn't an abandoned house. We drove around looking for the scene and couldn't find anyone. We tried calling Rescue on the radio but no one responded. I was getting upset.

Finally, Rescue radioed us and directed us to where they were - 4 blocks further from the second location! I grumbled, "This is ridiculous!" As we finally pulled up, I watched Rescue try to intubate this guy without luck. I walked up and asked "What do we have guys?" They said, "We don't know. We think it is an assault."

It was an assault alright! The man had major lacerations on the right side of his head, his face was all black and blue, his right chest wall was all black and blue, his abdomen was rigid, his arms were all scraped and cut up. I asked, "What are his vitals?" One of the Rescue guys said, "I'm having a hard time getting a blood pressure. I think it's 70 or 80 by palpation. His pulses were around 100. I asked, "Is he breathing?" They said, "He was when we got here." Then it dawned on me, they had been on scene 20 minutes before us and hadn't gotten anything done. I thought to myself, "This man is dying and we're going to lose him unless we act fast." I said to Nancy, "grab our stuff. I need the pneumatic anti-shock trousers (M. A. S. T.), jump bag and ECG monitor."

As Nancy ran to the ambulance to collect our gear, I had Rescue start ventilating the patient with a bag-valve-mask, while I set up to intubate the patient. I had the other Fire Department rescue paramedic hook up the monitor, which showed a heart rate of 70 beats per minute in a normal sinus rhythm. I took the rescue crews laryngoscope and tried to intubate the patient, but the batteries were low and I couldn't see anything. I then grabbed their bag-valve-mask and started ventilating. I said, "listen to the breath sounds and tell me what you hear." One of the rescue guys replied, "both lungs are pretty much equal. A lot of junk down there though." Just as I had figured. He had aspirated a lot of stuff into his lungs. Nancy was starting an IV and I said to her, "As soon as you're done, let's get him into the ambulance. He's going downhill." She inserted the line, taped it down and was ready to roll by the time I got the words out of my mouth. We loaded the patient onto the cot and put him into our ambulance. Rescue was wandering around like a bunch of lost souls. Once in the ambulance, I grabbed my laryngoscope blade and intubated the patient. As I looked at the monitor I noticed a rate of 30 bpm. As the rescue paramedic stepped into my ambulance, I said, "Check for a pulse." Rescue said, "He's still got a pulse." I said, "yes but what is the rate?" He answered, "30". "You'd better start CPR," I replied. We radioed into the hospital and advised who we were transporting.

By the time we reached the hospital, the patient's pulse rate had picked up enough that we stopped CPR. I later learned that he had a basal skull fracture and was bleeding internally but that they didn't know from where.

Life away from work

I've really become an outdoors nut lately. There's so much to do around here on my days off, that is if I'm not sleeping! I've become quite taken by the Nevada desert, and sneak out to enjoy it every chance I get. I love roaming through old mines and ghost towns. Not the ones that are publicized, but the ones that you have to hike to, or use a four-wheel-drive to reach. The desert is so beautiful. All you have to do is slow down long enough to see.

The other day, I hiked to the Potisi mine, an old mine that was closed over 20 years ago. I had driven out to the area, hiked up to it late in the afternoon, and was sitting on the mountain at sunset.

The Potisi mountain overlooks a beautiful little valley out in the middle of nowhere. As the sun was setting, the scenery was unlike any I've ever come across. The pastel sky, the ever-changing rock colors, and shifting shadows made a lasting impression on my mind. Places like this have become important for my sanity. They give me an opportunity to relax, unwind, and collect my thoughts on what I'm doing, where I'm going and can I handle what is happening in this job that deals with life and death decisions daily.

Another favorite location near the city of Las Vegas is Mount Charleston. It is a 9-mile hike to the 12,000 feet top of Mount Charleston. Once there, "what a view!" Mount Charleston is the second highest peak in Nevada. Being that high, not many people take the four to five hours hike to reach the peak.

When there's not enough time to get out into the desert, I have a couple of nightclubs that I like to go to. "Carlos Murphy's" is one of my favorites. They typically have crazy bands and the crowd is always friendly. The other location is a place called "The Brewery." It has a nice dance floor and a fun dancing crowd. Another nice thing about them is that I can go alone, dance the night away, have fun and not worry if my date is enjoying herself!

Shelley gave up trying to win me over for her own a long time ago and has just accepted the fact that she will only be a good friend. The truth is, I already have a love that no one can compete against. That first love is my work; Whenever she calls, I always answer. Even if I'm mad at her…

Back to work

Today, August 30, 1984, I'm again working with Nancy Martin. It seems that as of lately, I've been working with her almost exclusively. Nancy is not an easy person to work with and many paramedics try to change partners when they discover that she is assigned to them. I agree that she can be a pain in the butt from time to time, but she is a smart paramedic and I think I can learn a lot from her. Today we are working out of Substation 11, "the Las Vegas strip," This substation is typically run by EMT intermediates (not paramedics), and these teams typically get most of the non-emergent (code 2) calls, with a few emergent calls that happened along the Vegas strip. Simply put, it is a very busy substation with very little excitement.

The morning started off with two non-emergent hospital transfers from Sunrise hospital to Valley hospital, then a transfer from Valley hospital to Southern Memorial hospital. Those calls were followed by a "man-down" emergency call at the intersection of Eastern and Washington Boulevard. The day was turning into a real inconvenience, fast!

We finally slowed down long enough to grab a bite to eat at two in the afternoon. Sadly, our break was short-lived. We received a non-emergent hospital transfer from Henderson to Valley hospital for x-ray. Our evening continued to be as hectic as the day. Out of the 24-hour shift, I believe we only managed two hours of sleep.

8 AM, 31 August, 1984

Our shift ended on time, which was just time enough for me to jump into another ambulance taking a patient to Loma Linda University Hospital in Southern California (a 12 Hour Drive). Just before departing, my Supervisor - Dan Netski, waved us down and said, "I need this ambulance back in town by 4pm for another standby. I said, "Dan, do you know what you're asking of this ambulance? I can do it, but I don't think you really want to put this ambulance through that. Do you?" Dan just said, "Get this ambulance back here on time." I replied, "All right. You asked for it." Pete Vier was the other paramedic on this trip. Pete had also worked the night before. I looked over at Pete and said, "4 o'clock high?" Pete said, "4 o'clock... Want breakfast?" I answered, "Sure."

Our patient was at Sunrise hospital, so we pulled around to the back and slipped into the cafeteria. After eating breakfast, we loaded the patient into the ambulance and headed for Loma Linda California. Our patient was an elderly female with cancer. I was the attendant while Pete was the driver. Pete was cruising along at a pretty good pace while the husband of my patient was riding up front. I overheard him ask Pete, "How fast are we going? 70?" Pete just smiled and said, "Yeah". I think the old guy would have died if he knew our average speed was 90 miles an hour!

We made it to Loma Linda in just over three hours. I jumped out the back doors of the ambulance and said to Pete as I looked at my watch "Not too bad." We settled our patient into her room and flirted with a few of the nurses for a while. Pete asked, "Hungry?" I answered, "Sure".

We scooted back to our ambulance and headed off to find a restaurant for lunch. After lunch, I swung behind the wheel of the ambulance and headed for home. Pete strapped himself onto the ambulance gurney and went to sleep. Next time, I'm driving first!

My speed home was not any slower than Pete's. While en route home, I passed two new American ambulance Units, both had left Las Vegas hours before us. I just laughed, honked, and waved.

Our time back in town was 4:30 PM. The standby crew jumped in and took off with it. I said, "Be nice to her guys, she's gone through hell once already! Dan Netski just smiled and said, "Not bad." I smiled and said, "Good night Dan." It had been quite a long shift. I punched out and took it easy around the house for the rest of the day.

4 – MURDER AND MVA'S

18 September, 1984

Since I started working at Mercy ambulance, I've been partnered with almost every one that no one else wants to work with. Now it's Nancy Martin (again). She's another one that has problems playing nicely in the sandbox. I have managed to tolerate them all and in fact enjoyed working with most of them - up to a point. It was at that point, however, that they had to find someone else; usually a new employee that had no other choice.

September 16, 1984 was the beginning of the end for Nancy Martin and my partnership. On that day Nancy and I started our shift at 7 AM, working out of Substation 2 (the lower Vegas strip) and working out of ambulance Unit 86, (the most hated ambulance in the squad).

A few fellow paramedics walked up to me and told me that I had already three strikes against me when I came to work! Then things got worse! As we were checking our ambulance, one of my supervisors (John Stanton) came up to me and said, "Are you ready for this afternoon?" I said, "Ready for what?" He said "Your senior oral boards." I said, "My senior oral boards?! Thanks for letting me know in advance! I hope I'm ready." Strike 4!

I thought to myself, "Well, I'll try and review a little at our substation." No such luck. We went from call to call to call up until the time I went before my oral boards.

I was just a bit nervous as we pulled back into Station 1. Fortunately things went all right. My examiners were Dr. Homanski (ER Doc), Paramedic Sean McManus (Senior Paramedic for the Las Vegas Fire Department), and registered nurse Nancy Dunbar (ER Nurse and Paramedic Instructor); all good friends that I held professionally in high regard. I passed with flying colors.

My next station was the trauma station and I became very nervous when I saw a good friend of mine come out pale and sweaty. I thought, "Oh God! I'm going to die."

I walked in and sat down. They started shooting questions at me and I couldn't talk, my mouth was so dry that all my words stuck together. I was so embarrassed, but I made it through and passed my senior boards. Relieved that that was over, I went and found Nancy and we started back to work. We ran a couple of minor calls; a child that cut his hands and a woman that collapsed at the Dunes Hotel due to overexertion. (What we call "The Las Vegas Syndrome" or "Vegas Syndrome" for short, caused by too much partying and not enough sleep.)

Our next call was to meet an ambulance from Laughlin Nevada at the midway point in Searchlight Nevada (about 40 miles outside of Las Vegas). I was attending and Nancy was driving. It's quite a drive so Nancy and I just chatted about things in general. I learned that she was having trouble with her boyfriend and this gave her an opportunity to unload her frustrations on someone else. So I just sat back and listened. It's times like this, that I'm glad I'm not dating! We arrived to Searchlight before the other ambulance, so we went into a local restaurant and ordered a soda. While we were waiting, dispatch radioed to inform us that our patient wasn't doing well and that the Laughlin ambulance would be there in a couple minutes.

"No biggie I thought", the patient had to be basically stable before the hospital would consider transport. So I thought.

Laughlin ambulance Unit 92 pulled up alongside our ambulance. I walked to the back doors, opened them and saw an elderly woman that looked dead! I exclaimed, "Guys! Is she breathing?" They said, "Well, she was when we left." I said, "Let's get her into my ambulance!" As we were loading her from one ambulance to the other, I watched for respirations. She was breathing, but only eight times a minute. The other crew had inserted an oral pharyngeal airway which had frothy sputum coming out of it.

Once loaded into my ambulance, I started to work. "What's the reason for the transport?" I asked. "Renal failure with heart problems." Was the reply. "Meds? Allergies?" I asked. "We don't know." They replied, "I suppose it's all in the nursing notes." I said, "Thanks." They had started a lactated ringers IV and placed her on nasal cannula oxygen. This patient was messed up! Both her eyes were black and blue, as well as her chin. Her lower left and right abdominal quadrants had marked bruising, as well as her left side. She was unconscious and responding only to deep painful stimuli. Her ECG showed normal sinus rhythm with unifocal premature ventricular contractions (PVCs).

Her condition was worsening by the second and I decided to intubate her. I retrieved my laryngoscope blade and suctioned her mouth so that I could see her trachea. Just as I was about to slide the endotracheal tube into her windpipe, she coughed and I caught a face full of bloody sputum! Maintaining my composure, I still managed to slide the tube into place. Upon ventilating, her lung sounds were full of water. I suctioned the endotracheal tube of a large amount of frothy sputum and started positive pressure ventilations, which helped clear up and push the fluid out of her lungs. She finally started to get a little color into her face. By the time we arrived to the hospital, she had spontaneous respirations at around 20 breaths per minute and her PVCs were cut in half.

I had radioed ahead to tell the hospital who we were bringing and they set up a ventilator for her. The woman was obviously going into congestive heart failure and from the nurses' notes, it sounded like she had fallen two days ago and might also have a closed head injury. Definitely a sick lady. I was relieved to be able to turn her over to the hospital staff.

As the day wore on, we handled the typical load of non-emergent calls; drunks, and mental health, as well as the occasional *critical patient*. Around 1 AM we made it back to our substation (substation 2 at Desert Springs hospital). Thank God! Nancy was really starting to get grumpy!

At around 3 AM, we responded to a fire at the King Albert Motel (which is where Substation 11 is located.) While en route, I joked to Nancy, "What a way to get dispatched! "Substation 11, report to your ambulance. Your substation is on fire!"

It was my turn to drive. I headed up Flamingo Boulevard toward the King Albert Motel. While en route, we heard that Mercy ambulance Units 97, 87 and American ambulance Medic three were also being dispatched along with Fire Department Rescue Units 11 and 12.

As we approached the corner of Koval and Flamingo Boulevard, we heard Rescue 11 advise Mercy dispatch that the triage area would be on the west side of the building. I then proceeded up Flamingo Boulevard and turned in to the parking lot on the west side of the building behind Mercy ambulance Unit 90.

As we exited the ambulance, Mercy ambulance Paramedic Jim Cox (from Unit 90 and my former roommate) was carrying a young boy towards us. I opened the back doors of our ambulance, so the patient could be placed on our cot. The patient's chief complaint was ankle pain from jumping out of a second story window.

I asked Jim if there were any other patients. He advised that he thought there was a little girl from the same family. While Nancy examined the 11-year-old boy with the ankle injury in the back of our ambulance, I found the father holding the little girl Jim had mentioned. I asked him if she was alright, to which the father replied that she was. I did a quick physical exam and found the little girl in good health.

I then went to the back doors of our ambulance and asked Nancy if she was ready to go. She insisted that we weren't leaving with just one patient and to check around for more. I said, "Okay" and headed for Rescue 11. As I approached them, I asked, "Is this triage control?" They said, "Yes." I asked, "Do we have any more patients?" They stated there were none at this time, but they were doing a room to room search. I said, "Okay, we'll take off with the one we have." They said "Let us know where you are transporting to." I said, "Okay". I went to my ambulance and closed the side doors, and then went around to the back of the ambulance and advised Nancy that there were no more patients and again asked if she was ready to go. She said, "No" and then asked if we had any ace wraps. I said, "I don't believe so." She said, "Check under the front jump seat." Which I did, but there were none.

Robin Nunn from American ambulance medic two, came by and asked why we were still on scene. To which I replied, "Nancy needs an ace wrap." Robin went to the back of my ambulance. Nancy asked her to look in medic two for an ace wrap, but Robin declined. I approached Robin and asked if she had found an ace wrap to which she replied, "No". She then asked me why Nancy needed one. I said, "we have a kid with an ankle." Robin then asked, "what's the matter with kerlix bandages and cardboard splints?" I said, "It's Nancy's patient." I then went to the back of my ambulance and advised Nancy that there wasn't an ace wrap in medic two. While at the back doors, I noticed Nancy palpating the patient's foot. The family was from Israel, spoke very little English, and all of Nancy's poking and prodding on this kids foot was upsetting the entire family.

I again asked Nancy if she was ready to go, to which she snapped "No!" By this time, I was becoming more upset. Mercy Unit 90, rescue 11, and American medic two all asked me why we were still on scene. I just said, "Nancy's not ready yet." The patient's father also kept asking why we weren't going. Frustrated, I got in behind the steering wheel and leaned back to look at Nancy in the rear and said, "Let me know when you are ready to go." The Fire Department paramedics were also walking to the back of our ambulance and told Nancy that she *was* going! Nancy then popped her head up through the front opening, and advised me that we were ready to go and that Fire Department would help me back up. Nancy then said that the reason we had stayed so long was because we were waiting to be cleared to leave by the Fire Department command. I just shook my head. Mercy Supervisor Unit 87 was just pulling onto the scene as we departed. I decided I'd give him a call once we arrived at Sunrise hospital to pass my frustrations about this call.

Once we had delivered this very stable patient to the emergency room, Nancy laid into me again. She chastised me stating that at standbys, you have to find the fire control and the triage station, so as to know where to park the ambulance, where patients are to be taken and when we can leave. I told her that I had talked to the triage and control and that they had indeed cleared us to leave. Nancy retorted, "They are not in charge! You have to talk to the fire captain!" I just shook my head and said, "That's ridiculous". I went and restocked the equipment we used and then went to the phone and called Dan Netski (the shift supervisor).

Dan was away from his car phone, so I had dispatch get a hold of him and had him call me at the Sunrise hospital emergency room. Dan called the ER, and Nancy picked up the phone. He asked her what she wanted, and she said she didn't want anything. I said, "If that's Dan, I want to talk to him." She handed me the phone and I said, "Dan, Nancy's been telling me that we can't leave the scene of a fire without the approval of the fire chief, which I think is ridiculous." Dan said, "That's bull shit, when we're on-scene, we take care of the patients and the firemen fight the fire." He also told me he had heard about what had happened prior to his arrival at the scene and that he was going to talk to Nancy in the morning. I said, "Thanks Dan." Nancy said, "Let me talk to him," but he had already hung up so she called his phone back and started in on him! While I don't know the extent of the conversation I'm sure Dan gave her an earful! When Nancy got off the phone she again laid into me. "What the hell are you trying to do? Get me in trouble? All Dan did was yell at me! You're such a fuck head!" I said, "Wait a second. If he yelled at you, it's your own doing. I called just to confirm the fact that you were feeding me bull shit!" Nancy said, "You're nothing but a fucking back stabber!" I said, "bull shit! Don't go blaming your mess ups on me! If I was going to be a back stabber, I'd have waited until later. My call to Dan was to confirm policy. In other words, Nancy, I didn't believe a word of what you were telling me on scene!"

We drove back to our substation not uttering a word to each other. As we got out of the ambulance, Nancy said, "And you can find yourself another partner, because I'm not working with you! I smiled and said, "That can be arranged." Fortunately, we only had one more call before we got off shift.

A hitchhiker was walking along Boulder Highway, and was struck by a car, knocked into the air, and then hit by second car, knocked up into the air again, and then run over by a third car before coming to rest in a bloody heap on the highway. Obviously he was dead before we arrived on scene. I don't think he even felt the third car. We cleared from this call and headed back to station one.

As I got out of the ambulance I said, "Nancy, as I say to all my partners at the end of the shift, it's been a REAL inconvenience. I'll take care of that request you made last night."

As I've said before, I live by a basic rule. I'm behind my team 100% and will give you the benefit of the doubt, but once I've hit my limit, you are on your own! Nancy was about to discover that she had hit that limit.

Our shift ended at 7 AM, but Dan didn't get off until 8. Since Nancy had to be in class by 8 AM, I had Dan all to myself when he arrived at station one.

"Dan," I said, "I have a little problem that I need to discuss with you." He said, "Let me guess, your little problem is named Nancy Martin." I said, "You got it." I explained to Dan what happened, relating word for word what I had said and what Nancy had replied. Dan asked, "Where is she?" I said, "She wasn't going to wait around for you. She went to her classes." Dan fumed, "That bitch! I told her I wanted to see her in my office this morning!" I said, "Well I guess Dan, she must think more of her school than she does of her job." Dan said, "Maybe a few days off will make her appreciate her job more." I just smiled and said "Whatever you think is right Dan. Oh by the way, Nancy said that she never wanted to work with me again. Do you think you could arrange that for me?" Dan smiled and said, "Sure, if I had my way she wouldn't work with anyone. EVER." I thanked Dan.

Having fully vented to my supervisor, and feeling vindicated, I headed home.

9 AM Wednesday, 19 September, 1984

After a short nap, I cleaned the house and then worked on my newly purchased 1969 International Scout 4 x 4. This new purchase was going to be my weekend Rest and Relaxation mobile, but I needed to be sure it didn't strand me out in the desert!

Just before noon, I headed off to the PGA Golf Tournament.

My friend, Dennis Nolan, had the EMS contract for the Las Vegas

PGA golf tournament, and had asked for volunteers to support him at the Desert Inn golf course. I had never attended a professional golf tournament and jumped at the opportunity. I was teamed up with Mercy ambulance paramedic, Craig Heins, and given a tricked out ambulance golf cart!

All the world-class golfing pros were expected to be there today and we had access to the full course!

Being a novice to professional golf, I didn't recognize any golf stars, but Craig knew quite a few and pointed them out to me as we traversed the course. While Craig was excited to see and meet them, I was just enjoying the warm fall day and taking in the beauties that lined the course.

8 AM Thursday, 20 September, 1984

I'm working with Paul Young on American - Medic two. The day began extremely slow, so Paul and I just hung around the substation and slept most of the morning. Seems like when I work the American ambulance shifts, all that the patients want is our opinion on whether they should go to the hospital or not. For instance, we had a woman that had been working harder than usual around the house. She hadn't eaten or drank anything for the past six hours and passed out. I said, "Ma'am, what do you expect? It's your body's way of saying slow down!"

The afternoon was equally as slow. We had a couple patients that had fallen, and a few auto accidents where no one needed transport. In fact, it was nice to get off shift and still feel refreshed!

8 AM Friday, 21 September, 1984

I headed back to the Desert Inn golf course to work the PGA golf tournament again. Today, they would have both PGA Pros plus movie stars playing. I am working with an EMT volunteer from Dennis Nolan's group named Paula. Paula met me at the front gate, and we headed for the other end of the course to see who we could see. The first star we saw was Gary Morris, a TV star from shows like "Mission Impossible" and "Ironsides". He wasn't playing very well and told us that if he shot any worse he was going to take a dive and have us get him out of there! We laughed and said, "For a nominal fee, all things are possible."

The next VIP we saw was Lee Trevino, a Class A pro golfer. Mr. Trevino was an extremely nice guy with a great sense of humor, which was a good thing since he was playing pretty lousy golf! The last person we met was Claude Akins who played Sheriff Lobo on the TV show "BJ and the bear." I was impressed. He played excellent golf and was easy to talk to. He made an attempt to remember everyone's name he met. The weather was again fantastic; blue skies; about 95° with a gentle breeze.

I left the tournament at 5 PM and went home to sleep. I had a date that evening with a Sunrise hospital secretary and we were going to the Tropicana Casino to see the Follies Bergère show.

The evening was fantastic. The show was great, and we went nightclub hopping until 3 AM. I was in bed by 3:30 AM (alone!) and back to work at 6 AM.

Surprise, surprise! It was with my favorite partner, Nancy Martin.

7 AM Saturday, 22 September, 1984

Fortunately, I had had enough time to cool down to tolerate Nancy for maximum of 24 hours. (That is if she could keep her mouth shut) I made it into work and stepped into the dispatch office to confirm I indeed had to work with her. Unfortunately, I did.

We were scheduled to work out of Unit 81. I grab the keys as Nancy came through the dispatch doors. I said, "Nancy, here are your keys." She said, "To what?" I said, "To your ambulance." She asked, "Who am I working with?" I said, "Me." She said, "Well, you'll have to find someone else to work with. You told Dan that you didn't want to work with me." I said, "Nancy, you forget that was your request. The schedule has us listed working together and I thought I could tolerate you for maximum of 24 hours, but I'll get that changed." Dan Netski was just getting to work and I said, "Dan we have a problem this morning." Dan said, "I know and I'll get you to split."

To my great fortune, I was given Rick DeCosta as my new partner. We readied our ambulance and headed for downtown Las Vegas to Substation 3.

As we drove to the substation, I told Rick about my morning's escapades. He replied, "I'm surprised you put up with her for as long as you did. I have no love for the woman and neither does anyone else in the company." Rick is a jolly fellow and as easy going as they get, and to have him say that about someone else reassured me that I was not the one out of line. We were extremely busy all day long. It was one of those days that turned into one of those evenings, that turned into one of those mornings.

The first call of the day was at the corner of First and Ogden Street, for a man with chest pain. We arrived on scene and found Mr. John Blue. Mr. Blue was a very well-known homeless guy that lived in and around the Las Vegas strip. Mercy ambulance had transported him hundreds of times to the hospital for various reasons. We knew that if we didn't transport Mr. Blue to the hospital, we would receive a half dozen more calls concerning him until we did. There is never anything wrong with John, other than the fact that he is an unrepentant drunk.

As Rick and I exited the ambulance and walked to the scene, the rescue guys jokingly said to Rick, "It's your dad, Rick!" And at that very instant, John saw Rick and said, "Ricky, my boy! How you doing son?" Rick just laughed and said, "What's wrong John?" John said, "Awe, I'm just drunk. I'm going to go find a place to sleep." Rick said, "Come on John, let's go to the hospital." John agreed and we slung him over our shoulders and dragged him to the back of the ambulance and put him onto the stretcher.

John then started in on the 100th rendition of "You know I was a Major in the Army." We'd say, "Yes John we know, we know!" We transported John to Southern Nevada Memorial Hospital (So. Ma. Mo.) and dropped him off. John was a very familiar sight to the staff there as well, and was escorted to his usual room for drying out.

Rick and I departed the hospital for another call. A "man down" at Third and Carson Street. This guy had just been released from Southern Memorial hospital and was driving home and had a stroke. I asked the man, "What were you admitted for last time?" "Seizures," he said. I said, "Well partner, it looks like you're going to get to visit them again." We took him back to So. Ma. Mo. hospital and dropped him off.

At shift change, the out-going crew hadn't filled the ambulance with gas, so we took the opportunity to tank the Unit up while the call volume was slow. It was a good thing we did, because at about 11 AM we started running back-to-back calls.

We responded from one automobile accidents to the next, then to an elderly man that fell off a roof, and then to an overdose of Motrin and Tylox.

At about 6 PM, we started running on assault calls. Our first assault was for a couple of guys that were sitting at a red light, when the truck behind them stopped. Two guys jumped out, ran up to them and started punching them. When it was all over, one guy had a laceration on his head, another was beaten on the head and shoulders with a lead pipe, and the rest had multiple scrapes and abrasions. I never did hear how that all started. Road rage, I guess.

As the evening progressed we received a call for a black woman that had told her common law husband that he was lazy and never did anything. Well, to prove she was wrong, he slapped her around their apartment for a while!

Our next call was like a remake of an old Three Musketeers flick! We received the call for a knifing in the projects on the northwest side of town. The buildings in this particular housing project formed a rectangle with all the apartments opening up to a central courtyard or square. As we entered the courtyard we could hear screaming and yelling; glass breaking and pots and pans flying about. The lights in the entire apartment building complex were out except for one. As we were standing in the courtyard, listening to the commotion, a large black man approached us from behind. "Where is apartment 20?" asked Rick. The large black man just smiled and said in a Southern drawl, "Guess."

Apartment 20 was on the ground floor in the middle of the complex. The front door was open and all the windows had been broken out. As I looked into the apartment (from some distance away) I could see a rather large black woman beating on the door with a bloody object that looked like a sword! There was blood everywhere; on the walls, floors, ceiling, and furniture. Suddenly, the door that the black woman had been beating upon flew open and another black woman emerged with her own large knife. The two then began their rendition of a sword fight from "the Pirates of Penzance." These two women were really whacking at each other. I stood and watched in amazement as these two women stabbed, and whacked at each other with their bloody knives.

While Rick and I stood there watching, I suddenly realized a crowd was gathering behind us. The large black man came alongside me and asked, "ain't ya'all gonna break'em up?" I said, "Man they don't pay me enough to do things like that!" I then asked Rick if the Metro Police Department had been called, and if not to ask them to please expedite. By this time, everyone that lived in that complex was out in the courtyard, and I think they were calling their neighbors over as well. We are talking about 1000 blacks in one of the poorest black projects. Probably not the best place for two unarmed white guys. I casually leaned over to Rick and whispered, "Did you lock the doors to the ambulance?" He said in a hushed shaky whisper, "Yes."

The Metro police finally showed up with three squad cars and two K-9 Units. By this time, the swashbuckling women were starting to get pretty tired of swinging at each other, and it wasn't too difficult to convince them to stop. Rick and I then split them up and started patching them up. I chuckled to myself, this reminded me of work on the mink farm back in Iowa! While both had several pretty good lacerations, I was surprised that none were life threatening.

Rick was caring for one lady in the kitchen, while I patched the other up in the living room. Thinking that the situation had calmed down, the police officers started asking questions about what happened. Having caught their second wind, the questions rekindled their anger and they started back at it again, this time out in the courtyard.

In the courtyard, the situation took a serious turn. The ladies now had an audience and it sounded like a football game during homecoming. As the police attempted to get the situation under control, the crowd turned ugly and began to riot. Some attacked the police, while others took one lady's side or the other. Rick grabbed his patients and started dragging her back into the house, while I grabbed my patient and tried dragging her toward the ambulance.

I was amazed that once I had managed to get my patient out of the courtyard and into the ambulance, she quickly calmed down and allowed me to re-bandage her wounds. The scene in the courtyard was going from bad to worse. Rick decided it was no longer safe to stay in the house with his patient and quickly returned to the ambulance. Rick jumped into the driver seat and started the ambulance. He said, "The police can bring the other patient to the hospital when she gets done fighting with them." With that, he put the ambulance in drive and we headed for the hospital, and civilization.

While en route, I asked this woman what all the fighting was about. She proceeded to tell that she was from California and that her brother lived in the apartment where the fighting took place. She had been staying at a friend's house in the same complex and had stopped by her brother's apartment to visit him.

Apparently, her brother would introduce her to several of his friends when she was "in need of a man." This evening she had knocked on the door and her brother's wife had let her into the apartment. The wife (her sister in-law) then closed and locked the door. She then turned and let her husband's sister have it, saying that she was sick and tired of her whoring around the project. She demanded that the woman leave and never show her face there again. My patient then explained to her in 'ghetto vernacular' that she had no intention of leaving, and how dare she tell her that she could not visit her own brother.

The verbal exchange then turned into a physical attack with both women being thrown around the inside of the apartment. The windows were broken, and furniture crushed. When my patient had been thrown into the kitchen, she thought she could scare the other woman away with a large butcher knife, but the other woman quickly produced a larger Bowie knife, and the Three Musketeers act began.

While the patient told me her tale, I thought to myself, "I wonder what the other lady is telling the police?" Once the woman finished her story, I just shook my head and said "It sounds like a full evening to me." She ended by saying, "All I wanted was a little luv'in." I said, "Lady, there are easier ways to get laid!"

We transported this fine upstanding lass to So. Ma. Mo. hospital and were en route back to our substation when we received a call for a shooting. The initial report was that two people had been shot on Rancho Circle Road (which is one of the wealthiest neighborhoods in Las Vegas). Unit 87, Rescue 3, and Metro police were also responding. We were the furthest Unit from the call and the last Unit to arrive. This particular road had no streetlights, in order to highlight the expensive lighting that each house displayed. The road also ran in a circle - One way in and one way out. I was driving and as we made our way around the circle I said to Rick, "Do you see any house numbers?" Rick said, "No, just look for the other Units. They should all be here ahead of us." As we continued on around the circle, I initially spotted a squad car, but couldn't see anyone. As our headlights settled on the squad car, I noticed everyone crouched behind their vehicles and ambulances. The police had their guns drawn and we were in plain sight of the house. I said, "Oh God. We're gonna die."

The scene reminded me of a call I had run while working in Sioux City, Iowa. During that call, I had responded to a domestic disturbance call. As my partner (Jim Black) and I descended a long hill to the scene, I saw police officers crouched behind their vehicles. As that imaged registered in my mind, two flashes erupted from the house, followed by two bullet holes in the windshield between my partner and I. I'm glad there was no one behind us, because Jim put that ambulance into reverse and accelerated at full speed back over the hill!

At today's scene, I quickly shut off all our lights; killed the engine; and exited the ambulance, using it to block me from the house. As I peeked around the ambulance, I could see a man lying in the driveway with what looked like a shotgun next to him. I could also see police officers creeping up alongside the house. I then heard the night supervisor say, "Ty... Ty, back your Unit up." I said, "Do what? Are you crazy? Are you trying to get me shot?"

Just then, a Metro police squad car shined a spotlight on the front door and shouted "Police!" and ordered the occupants of the house to come out and walk towards the light. From this million-dollar home emerged two 13-year-old girls. One lived there (Jessica Malin), and the other was a friend just spending the night (Sandy Shaw). Sadly, they would be the only two survivors of this nightmare.

The girls did what they were told and walked to the squad car where the light was coming from. I took care of the girls, while my partner and the other Units looked for more casualties. The girls were covered in blood. I didn't have to enter the house to know what happened. The two girls had been eyewitnesses to everything that had happened. Jessica, the girl that lived there, described everything. She said, "My mom (Virginia Malin) and her new husband (Alex Egyed, a Hungarian self-made millionaire) had gotten into a terrible fight earlier today out on the golf course at a charity event. She left him at the golf course and came home separately with some friends. When she arrived home, she woke up my friend Sandy and I, telling us to get some clothes together that we were all going to a friend's house for the rest of the night. That's when Alex came to the house. He was acting like a wild man. Throwing things all around the house, and knocking over furniture." The teen related that her mom had entered her room saying, "Come on we're going now."

"That is when he shot her. Right in the head." The young girl burst into tears and said, "I saw it all. I saw him kill my mother, and then he pointed the gun at me! I was so scared. I screamed and we ran into an adjacent bedroom and hid in the bathroom. He never came after us though. Then we heard two more shots and a car take off real fast. Then another shot. After that, the house was real quiet and we could hear sirens off in the distance. I finally snuck back into my room, and there was my mom, laying in a pool of blood and her friend (Jack Levy) was dead in the hall with a bullet hole in the head. My aunt (Betty DiFiore) was also dead in the living room. How could this happen to us? Why?!"

What do you tell a 13-year-old girl that has experience the most graphic form of violence available to man? Violence inflicted upon her own family. You can't! You can't say a thing, because nothing will remove the pain, the scars, the horror.

The other ambulance crews emerged from the house and confirmed what the young girl had told me. From what my partner gathered, the husband (a high tech computer businessman and owner of the house) shot all three people, then shot himself. I sat with the two girls while the police made a full check of the house. The emotional scars left on these two girls would be tremendous if they didn't get proper psychological evaluation. The permanent outcome could be devastating. Jessica looked at me and said, "Where are they going to take us?" I said, "Well I'm not sure. I know they're going to want you to tell them what happened. Do you have any other relatives in town?" She said, "Well my dad lives in town." I said, "I'm sure that's where you'll spend the night." Her friend, Sandy, said, "I want to stay with her, okay?" I said, "I think that can be arranged, but I think we better call your folks and let them know you're alright. If the news stations gets a hold of this story before you call them, your folks will go crazy with worry."

A female Metro police officer came over to the ambulance and took the girls to her squad car, and then headed for the police station to notify family members. I had a real sick feeling inside. Not for the dead victims, but for the survivors.

Just then dispatch broke my train of thought with "Unit 81, Control. Can you clear and copy another code 3?" I said, "10-4. Rick, we've got another call." Rick jumped into the ambulance and wrote down the call, and we were off.

It was another assault. A woman assaulted by her boyfriend's father. The assailant had come over to their house extremely intoxicated and when the woman tried to get him to sleep it off at their apartment before driving to his home, he beat her about her head and shoulders with a telephone and then ransacked the apartment. He then drove off for his home to beat up on his wife before calling it an evening. Metro police came and took the report, and then went over to his house and hauled him away to jail.

After we had delivered this patient to the hospital, I said to Rick, "Rick will this evening ever slow down?" Rick just shook his head and said, "It really is becoming a pain in the ass." I was beginning to run on fumes when we received our next call, "Bonanza and Mohave Avenue, woman in labor." I said, "Wonderful. That's all I need to do is deliver a baby at 5 AM in the morning!" Of course we were the first team to arrive on scene. Everyone else had at least made it back to their substations, which added to their delay in responding. As we entered the house, the husband and family were very calm It made sense, this was her 8th child and possibly her 3rd delivery by paramedics! I examined her and determined that delivery was close, but not imminent. We loaded her into the ambulance and headed for the hospital. While en route, I asked her if her water had broken. She replied "No", it usually breaks right at the time of delivery." I said, "Well hopefully that will be in labor and delivery at the hospital and not in the back of my ambulance." She delivered five minutes after we dropped her off in the labor and delivery Unit. Relief!

It was daylight now, Rick and I were beat! We went back to our substation and grabbed our gear, which we had last seen yesterday morning. From there, we headed back to Station 1 to clean our rig and go home for a well-deserved rest.

23 September, 1984

There comes a time when the body needs to recharge. My body was telling me it needed rest. I don't remember driving home; I don't remember getting undressed; I don't remember unplugging the phone or setting the alarm for 8 AM the next day. All I remember was going to sleep and being awakened by the alarm clock the next day.

24 September, 1984

Today is my day off and I needed to get a few things done around the house. I started a load of laundry, cleaned the yard, and replaced a radiator hose on my 1969 International Scout. I then drove downtown and bought a roll bar for the Scout. What a pain that thing was to install! I had to take off the back wheels and both gas tanks! What was initially thought to be an easy install, turned into an all-day affair that required replacing a lot of parts. Fortunately, it was all back together by sunset and I was able to drive it to a friend's house to watch a movie on her VCR machine.

6 AM Tuesday, 25 September, 1984

The telephone rang. I answered and heard, "Hello Ty? This is Nancy. Nancy Martin. I know you were sleeping and all, but do you think we could work together again? I'm really sorry for what I said. I said, "I don't know. We'll talk about it later. I'm working with Dan Netski today and you're working with Dennis Nolan." She said, "Well, okay. I'll talk to you later. Bye." I hung up the phone thinking to myself, "I don't believe this! One day she calls me every foul thing under the sun and the next day she expects everything to be hunky-dory?!"

By 8 AM. I was at work and preparing to team up with Mercy ambulance supervisor Dan Netski. Dan is Mercy ambulance's best shift supervisor; he is also my bowling partner, but more importantly a good friend. Dan and I always have a great time working together. I told Dan about my 6 AM phone call and related that I was not inclined to work with Nancy today. Dan replied, "I don't think anyone else is either!"

Fortunately they did not make me work with Nancy. The shift would turn out to be extremely slow with only six calls, and all minor; a twisted ankle here and a small laceration there. Boy Scout first aid stuff.

The end of the shift also held a small surprise for me. I received an award from the 'big boss', Bob Forbus (Mercy Ambulance Executive Director) for (and I quote) "Outstanding work in the field; Your high school drunk driving lectures, and for being able to put up with Nancy Martin! I hereby award you with the certificate of 'Employee of the Month'." I just laughed and said "Thanks Bob".

9 AM Wednesday, 26 September, 1984

After my surprise award ceremony, I headed home and became very lazy. I lounged around the house and did nothing until about 2 PM. I then went down to my credit union and applied for a credit card which took almost two hours. Afterward, I drove down to Lake Mead. It was a very nice day with a cool breeze. I used up a full tank of gas just driving around the lake and taking in the sights.

That evening was bowling night. The bowling crew met in the bowling alley bar at 8 PM. Bowling didn't start until 9 PM. After a few rounds of drinks, we were all primed for the match! We won! I don't know how, but we did and had a really good time doing it.

7 AM Thursday, 27 September, 1984

I tell you, this company sure knows how to push a guy to his limits! I'm working with Nancy Martin today out of substation 11 (Downtown). We are in Unit 86, the oldest ambulance on the streets. As I readied the ambulance, other paramedics at Station 1 would just shake their heads and say, "Dude, you have 3 strikes against you! Bad partner, bad ambulance, and bad district!" I just answered, "You're not hearing any argument from me!"

Nancy knew I was not happy and was trying her best to keep the conversation light and happy. We readied the ambulance and then headed for the streets. Even with the light chatter, there was still plenty of tension in the air and I really wondered how the day would turn out. We stopped by Sunrise hospital for breakfast and chatted with the crew from Unit 82. Paramedics Don Abshire and John Adams were the crew manning that Unit. Don was extremely upset over the new substation hours which ran from 7 AM to midnight. Don said that it came to a loss of $45/day and that he was very unhappy about being stuck there. Then Nancy made the suggestion, "I have school in the morning and a major test. I'd love to be able to get off at midnight to get a good night's rest and be ready for my test." Don looked at Nancy in amazement! He managed to stammer out, "I'll make some calls and see if I can't get us switched." Fifteen minutes later I was working with Don Abshire and couldn't be happier. I can't say that John was as thrilled as I was, however.

Don Abshire is a large, burly guy. He works hard, but he also plays very hard. At Mercy ambulance, folks either loved him or hated him. Not that it mattered much to Don. He was a good paramedic, but perhaps a little rough around the edges. That may have put some people off. Fortunately, Don liked working with me and I got along perfectly well with him.

Business out of substation 11 was steady. Our first call was for a woman that had collapsed at the Flamingo Hotel. She was a non-emergent transport to Sunrise hospital. This was followed by a non—emergent transport of a diabetic patient. The entire morning was spent delivering non-emergent patients from hospitals and homes to their required destinations.

Don is a good medic and quite the show off if something needs to be done. It doesn't matter to Don whether it needs to be done on the scene or in the ambulance, Don always prefers to do it on the scene. That evening, the call volume was exceptionally busy. Every time we returned to the substation another call kept our head from hitting the pillow. Once again, I watched the sunrise from the back of an ambulance. By 7 AM, I was ready to head home.

1 PM Friday, 28 September, 1984

I had promised Janet Smith (Mercy Ambulances Public Relations Coordinator and fellow paramedic) that I would do her a favor and take an ambulance over to the Marie Callahan elementary school and talk to the kindergarten class that was learning the alphabet. Of course, "A" stands for ambulance.

My little presentation to the class elaborated on the "A" theme: "A" stands for Miss "Ann" who had "Amnesia" from an "Accident" and can't remember the "Alphabet" and had to be brought in to the hospital by an "Ambulance." It would have been fantastic if I could have used an "American Ambulance," but such was not the case. I gave a little talk that I had concocted en route, shuttled the little rugrats through my ambulance, and answered extremely technical questions like, "How do you turn the siren on?" "What's that?" and "Are you a doctor?" By the end of the day, I was a hero to all and had 100 new best friends. To add a thrill to the day, I drove away with my red lights on and siren blaring.

I drove the ambulance back to Station 1 and let Janet know everything went well. I then jumped into my scout and headed for home. I had a ton of things to do. Number 1 on my list was cleaning my pool, which had mysteriously turned green again when I wasn't looking. The pool filters were all clogged and the pump was not running. I went down to my local pool combat center and picked up more supplies for my heavy chemical warfare against the green pool slime.

I then started cleaning the backyard. Black widow spiders were extremely thick around the backyard shrubs. Once again toxic chemicals were used to gain the upper hand on the arachnoid pests! That evening, I ran 4 miles through the neighborhood (while work is physically taxing, I've found that an evening jog through the neighborhood is very relaxing and helps me to sleep.) I then soaked in the Jacuzzi, and relaxed by the now sparkling clean and spider-free pool. I had to be at work the next day at 7 AM, replacing Craig Heins who wanted to go to a ski patrol class at the Mount Charleston ski lodge. I agreed to work part of his shift for him, 7 AM to 5 PM.

7 AM Saturday, 29 September, 1984

Craig's regular partner is Allen Skillen. Allen is a brand new paramedic fresh out of the Clark County Community College course based in Las Vegas. Allen is a "tall drink of water," standing a little over 6'5", with a black belt in Kung Fu. While a formidable image, Allen is a gentle soul. He has an easy-going personality and absolutely loves his new career as a paramedic.

Alan and I arrived to work at the same time, but nobody knew which ambulance we were supposed to be in. Once the proper ambulance was located, we had to scrounge around for supplies. The monitor and defibrillator were missing, there were no narcotics, and the oxygen cylinder was empty. I told Allen, "Allen I don't need this kind of aggravation. I'm not even supposed to be working today!"

Once the ambulance was fitted with equipment and supplies, we headed for the streets. It didn't take long for the calls to start rolling in. Our first call was for an infant choking, but we were canceled before we arrived on scene. Our 2nd and 3rd calls also involved children choking. Must have been something in the water. But we never made it to any of these calls, which is not unusual. During these events a child gets a little piece of food stuck or inhales a little water, then turns blue for a second and the parents freak out and call for an ambulance. But then the infant quickly recovers, the parents are embarrassed and cancel the response.

By mid-morning Allen and I found ourselves downtown caring for a drunk that had fallen and hit his head. He was quickly followed by a lady that was a known diabetic that had not eaten since she arrived to town. We started an IV and gave her an ampoule of D 50 W. She immediately recovered and refused to go to the hospital.

Upon clearing from this call, we were requested to respond to Station 1 to pick up a ride-along EMT (Emergency Medical Technician). Her name was DiDi. She was a volunteer EMT from the Overton Nevada ambulance squad. Overton is an Unincorporated Town located in Clark County, Nevada. The town is on the north end of Lake Mead. DiDi related that her tiny ambulance squad ran an average of ten calls a month, which reminded me of when I volunteered for the Kingsley, Iowa ambulance in the area I grew up.

Our dispatchers know when we have a ride-along, and do their best to give those ambulances interesting calls for the benefit of the guest. Once back in service, our first call was to a motor vehicle accident. Upon arriving on-scene we learned that all the injuries were minor and no one requested transportation to the hospital. We had just cleared from this accident, when I heard Mercy Unit 87 dispatched to an automobile accident in Kyle Canyon, located at the base of Mt. Charleston. The details were sketchy and they were the only Unit responding. I chuckled out loud and said, "I'm glad it's them (Joanne Dixon and Jennifer Painter) going all the way out there for a call that they're not even sure exists." Allen agreed.

We were then dispatched to an assault. Upon arrival we found a 50-year-old male that had just arrived to town and hadn't eaten anything in eight days; drank only cheap Rum; and was too weak to take another step. I asked the Metro police officer, "Who called this in as an assault?" The police officer said, "Oh, security did. They said he looked "beat up." I chuckled, "Sure! By the elements of nature!"

His name was John. I said, "Come on John, it's time to go to the hospital for a little rest and relaxation." We placed him on the gurney and put him into the ambulance. In the ambulance, John was really starting to slip. So I ran a few quick checks and found his blood sugar low, but his heart okay. No trauma noted either. I started an IV, gave him a shot of B12 (Thiamine) and an amp of D 50 W. John woke up and was as good as new by the time we arrived to the ER..

As we returned to service, we heard an update on Unit 87's call. The accident had been verified and it was a bad one. Possibly three dead on scene and another five or six critical injuries. The Valley Flight For Life helicopter was en route. I looked over at Allen and said, if they have five critical patients, they won't have enough rigs to transport." Dispatch must have been reading my mind, for across the radio came "Mercy 83 (not my Unit) go 10-8, code 3, for a 401 with injuries, 5 miles off of the Tonopah Highway 1, Kyle Canyon Rd." I said, "Sounds like a bad one. I hope Joanne and Jennifer can handle the triage."

Unit 87 was just getting on scene when we (Unit 81) were dispatched for a diabetic coma. While en route to our call, Mercy 87 advised, "We have three dead and six critical patients, please send another Unit."

Every ambulance in the city had been listening to what was going on in the Canyon, and everyone wanted to go. All of a sudden Unit 83 came over the air, "we've been involved in an accident. We're 10-7 (out of service), we'll advise if there's any damage or injuries." Dispatch said, "10-4, please advise as quickly as possible." I said, "Shit!" We were the closest Unit to both Kyle Canyon and to Mercy 83's accident. I got on the radio and said, "Dispatch, Mercy 81 is at the expressway and Jones Boulevard, do you want us to divert?" Dispatch responded, "10-4. Respond to the 401 at Kyle Canyon." I said, "10-4". Our third rider was all excited. She had never responded to a mass casualty incident.

Fortunately, Unit 83 reported that there were no injuries and no major damage to the vehicles. Dispatch advised them, "10-4. Continue en route to your call." Mercy Units 90, respond code 3, 421, diabetic, this will be Mercy 81's call on Jones." Mercy Unit 90 went en route to our initial call.

As we approached the turnoff to Kyle Canyon, Unit 87 radioed us to advise that we would need our spinal precautions equipment. The

Valley Flight For Life helicopter had landed beside Mercy 87 just opposite the accident. What a mess! The accident had been a head-on collision between a 1984 Camaro and a Chevy Van. According to witnesses, the driver of the Camaro had been racing people down the hill and had passed a slower car, slipped off the curb and then over-corrected, causing him to slam head-on, at about 90 miles an hour, into the van. The van contained a family of five that had been heading up the mountain for a picnic.

There were four people in the Camaro, three of them had been killed instantly. The only reason the survivor lived was because she was surrounded by dead bodies. As we pulled up to this mass casualty scene, I remembered what I had been taught in paramedic school: *When you arrive on the scene of a major call, the first thing you need to do is take your own pulse.* In other words, take a deep breath, slow down, assess your surroundings, and build a plan. That is exactly what we did.

The spinning rotors of the EMS helicopter kept us from approaching the scene. Allen and DiDi grabbed their gear and headed for the triage area. As they made a wide berth around the helicopter, I took in the carnage of this horrible accident.

It was a ghastly sight, and one of the worst I had seen in a long time. The Camaro was crossways on the highway, blocking traffic in both directions. It was completely mangled. I couldn't even tell what type of car it was. I could see a body sheet draped over the bloody pulp sitting in the area of the driver seat. I saw another sheet covering another body lying half in and out of the front passenger seat, and a third sheet draped over a body on the highway.

The EMS helicopter crew was working on the only survivor of the car. She had multiple facial lacerations, a possible closed head injury, a rigid abdomen (from internal abdominal bleeding) and a broken leg.

Ringing the wrecked Camaro and van were two other ambulances, a fire truck, a rescue truck, the Flight for Life helicopter, three Nevada

Highway Patrol cars and two Las Vegas Metro police cars. Traffic had been stopped on both ends and a large crowd was gathering around the scene.

I turned my attention to the van. The van was tan in color, probably a 1980 Chevy, it was hard to tell. The front end of the van was completely demolished. The van was in a horseshoe shape, that wrapped around the driver side leading me to believe it took most of the impact. The passenger side of the van was split open. The front passenger door had been torn off and the sliding door was sprung open. As I walked towards the van, I noticed two paramedics working on a 4-year-old boy that had been sitting on the back bench seat of the van. He had been unrestrained and was propelled forward like a missile and ejected through the front windshield and was lying in front of the van between the two wrecked vehicles. I overheard one medic tell the other, "I think he has a left femur fracture and possibly a lower back fracture. He also has multiple lacerations about his face and arms, and probably a closed head injury. Luckily he was unconscious, I don't think he could stand the pain if he was awake. He needs to go to the hospital now!

I then heard a voice shout, "Ty, we've got one coming out and she's yours." I said, "Okay. I've got a backboard ready to put her on." There was a bunch of movement inside the van and then the firemen handed out a 9-year-old girl. She was awake and shrieking in pain. While the Fire Department rescue team had placed a cervical collar on her neck, they were just carrying her out in their arms! As I placed my hand on the little girls thigh, I felt bones grinding together. I looked up at the rescue medic in horror and said, "My God man! She's got a broken femur! You can't just carry her out like that!" I then grabbed hold of her broken leg and pulled traction on it, which alleviated a lot of her pain. I then told the rescue medic to grab the Sager traction splints (a device that will help maintain leg traction for a femur fracture). While they were off looking for the traction splints, I started my assessment of the little girl. I determined that she had a black and blue abdomen, which was also as hard as a board, indicating internal abdominal bleeding. She also complained of neck and back pain, and was having difficulty breathing. Her level of consciousness was also dropping along with her blood pressure. The rescue medic returned with the traction splints. With the aid of a bystander, I secured the young child's leg to the traction device. I then started two large IVs and placed the girl into M.A.S.T. trousers (medical anti-shock trousers). I looked around and asked, "Where's the EMS helicopter crew? This one needs to go now!" They had just finished loading the 4-year-old boy into the helicopter when the flight medic came to my patient with their second stretcher. I told him what I had found and what I had done and turned the patient over to him.

I then looked over the shoulder of a paramedic that was working on the mother of this family. It appeared she was the only one wearing a seatbelt at the time of the accident. The impact was so hard that it ejected her out the side door of the van while still secured to her bucket seat! She was also critical with internal injuries, but not as bad as her two children.

The flight crew finished loading the two kids and had taken off for Sunrise hospital. In a moment of silence after the helicopter had departed, I heard a cry that I will never forget. It wasn't a loud cry, nor a top-of-your-lungs cry, nor was it a scream. It was the kind of sickening cry of a man that was completely conscious and completely hurt. The kind of cry that turns your stomach and makes you feel real queasy inside. This cry had come from the father of this family. The driver of the van.

Paramedic Jennifer Painter had been working on this guy since she arrived on scene. He was a mess. Jennifer hollered for me to give her a hand. As I climbed into the van, I stuck my hand in a bowl of potato salad. You can't imagine what a nauseating feeling it is to stick your hand into something cool and Gooey with all this trauma and carnage around you. For an instance, all I could think about was getting this mystery substance off my hand!

A moment later, I had regained my composure and was back on earth ready to take on my next patient. The father was suffering from multi-system trauma. He had taken the brunt of the accident. The entire dashboard had been shattered to bits. The steering wheel was broken; and the engine had come up into the cab and had sprayed him with hot oil and radiator fluid.

You couldn't even tell it was the front of the van. The metal rod under the gas pedal had gone through his left foot and had to be cut before we could remove him from the van. His right foot was only attached by a few tendons and a piece of flesh. Both his femurs were broken. He had a dislocated fracture of his left elbow and an open fracture of his right upper arm. He also had nine fractured ribs and a broken jaw. There were also multiple deep lacerations across his skull and a possible skull fracture.

I was amazed that this man was still alive, let alone awake! He knew where he was, what had happened, and he felt every twinge of pain from every broken bone. While a single broken bone is one thing, 17 broken bones is simply unbearable. As we began the extrication process, I could see it was taking its toll. We could no longer get a blood pressure and he was starting to become very pale and clammy. His veins had collapsed and we couldn't get an IV started. I said, "Time to roll guys. He can't wait." We rapidly extricated him from the vehicle and loaded him and his wife into my ambulance. We tried once again to start an IV in the ambulance, but even with M.A.S.T. pants inflated, we couldn't get his blood pressure up.

DiDi, Jennifer, and Alan stayed in the back of the ambulance to attend to the needs of the two critical parents. Time was of the essence, I needed to get these folks to our level I Trauma Center as quickly as possible. The road back into town was extremely congested and traffic was not helpful. It seemed like every jerk in town had to pull out in front of me or slam the brakes in order to slow us down. One particular fool on a motorcycle was stopped at an intersection; he literally looked at me with my red lights and siren on, and as I entered the intersection, purposely pulled out in front of me. My poor team in the back! I had to hit the brakes so hard that Jennifer came sliding up between the front seats. I begged forgiveness and tried to explain, but she was pissed. We arrived at the hospital with both parents in stable but critical condition.

The emergency room Doc. took one look at the father, ordered x-rays and shipped him off to surgery. The mother was found to have blood in her urine and was also rushed to surgery for a ruptured bladder.

After it was done and the sweat was finally slowing down, I looked into the back of our ambulance. It took only 20 minutes to trash it and will take 2 hours to clean up. You take a deep breath and say, "Things could have been better, but I think we did alright."

I cleaned out our ambulance and retrieved replacement supplies, and then drove our ambulance to the company mechanic. During the emergency drive to and from this accident, I managed to lose an engine belt. The mechanic didn't want to hear about the lives saved, all he cared about was the alleged abuse he thought his ambulance had endured.

Thirty minutes later (it could have been only 15 minutes later had the mechanic stopped his bellyaching) we were back in service and ready for the next call. As we drove onto the streets, I leaned back to our ride-along and said, "Well, has it been interesting enough for you?" She said, "I haven't ever seen anything like that in my life." I smiled and said, "Wait until we have a really good call!" She just shook her head. We almost made it to our substation when we were dispatched to another accident involving a bicycle and a car.

We arrived on scene to find a 10-year-old boy with a broken tibia-fibula fracture (lower leg). He had cut across the streets and was struck by a car and knocked 30 feet down the pavement. I'd say he was very lucky! We calmed him down and splinted his leg. The neighbors found his mom and we started en route to the hospital.

During the trip, I found out that this youngster wasn't even supposed to be where he was. He hadn't looked both ways when he crossed the middle of the street, and his behavior in the ambulance was unbecoming for a boy in as much trouble as he was!

I decided to educated him in the back of my ambulance. His mom was crying and very upset, and this little terror was trying to behave indifferently and say, "Who cares. I'm going to die anyway." I looked at him in a stern manner and said, "You're right." He then suddenly looked up at me with a worried expression.

Having gotten his attention, I said, "We are all eventually going to die, but if you keep pulling stupid stunts like the one you just did, it'll be a lot sooner than you think!"

We transported him and his mom to So. Ma. Mo. hospital. I finished my paperwork and headed for Station 1. It was 6 PM and I was ready to go home and crash. Craig Heins met us at the door and said, "Sure Ty, take all my good calls!" I smiled and said, "Someone had to, why not the best!"

Just as Craig jumped into the ambulance, they received another call to who knows where. I was glad to be off. I drove home, changed into my shorts and a T-shirt and puttered around the house.

At around 8 PM, as the day started to cool, I went out for my four mile run. As mentioned before, my evening runs had become integral to my mental health. Half the time I am amazed by what came bubbling to the surface during those runs.

After the run, I soaked in the Jacuzzi for an hour and then called it an evening. As I lay in bed, I thought about the family in the van. I thought about what happened to people that we take care of, that is after all the surgery is done and all the cast work is in place.

Surgeons can repair tissue and fix broken bones but they will never be able to repair what was torn out of this family. I imagine the father will have at least two years of rehabilitation ahead of him. The kids would be out of school for quite some time, and may suffer permanent disability.

Life is odd. Some people can go through it and hardly ever know what is real and what is make-belief. Others have to experience some of the hardest events life has to offer. I get to act as the mediator; trying to place some sort of order in some of life's most tragic and terrifying times. I really think paramedics need to visit psychologists every once in a while just to vent. I mean really good ones. I can tell a quack from a mile away. They need someone to sit down and talk to the guys about once a month and say, "How goes it?" Not because people are losing it, but to prevent people from losing it. Someone to help take some of the bite out of burn-out.

I'm 21 years old and have now been responding to pain, trauma and injury since I was 15 years old. Six years. I've seen older paramedics with six years' experience not do so well in managing their stress: Alcohol, drugs, abuse, broken marriages and emotional distancing.

Enough of this. Time to sleep. I've got work in the morning.

5 – WORK AND VACATION

8 AM Tuesday, 16 October, 1984

Time in Las Vegas has a tendency to slip by quickly and I find myself playing catch-up in my writing. Work has been heavy. There have been a few rather interesting calls, although the majority have been routine. I'll try to remember the more interesting ones.

A few days ago, I took care of my very first Russian! He was a chef at the Union Plaza Hotel. The call came in as a "man down". We arrived on scene and found an elderly male gentleman in the office of the main kitchen. A witness related that he just collapsed at work.

Upon our arrival, the patient was conscious and sitting in a chair. He didn't know who, what, or where he was. He acted extremely anxious and was very uncooperative. He kept jabbering in Russian and only his son could understand him. After questioning the son for as much info as we could about his father, we found out that he was a diabetic and had high blood pressure. The man was fairly large and it took four guys to hold him down while I started an IV and pushed and amp of dextrose. His blood sugar before the amp of dextrose was around 10, where 80 is normal. After the amp was given, he snapped right out of his disorientation and calmed down. We explained what had happened and what we had done.

He then spoke English with a very strong Russian accent, "Iss okay now? No?" His name was Baum Zornski, but I just called him "Boris." "Boris", I said "You have to go to the hospital and find out why your blood sugar dropped so fast." Boris answered, "My sugar iss fine now, no? I no need go, iss okay." I replied, "No Boris. Sugar is no fine. Boris goes to hospital now. Yes." After about 15 minutes of coaxing and prodding, we finally got Boris to the hospital, but he still signed himself out of the hospital, against medical advice. Oh well, you win some and you lose some. *Ruskis iss stubborn. No?*

Everyone at Mercy ambulance has been working extremely hard. My new roommate is Bob Cochran, a relatively new graduated from Paramedic school and working for Mercy full-time. He started dating Shelly Windholtz and the next thing I knew, she was living with us! I was happy for Bob. Shelly is a wonderful girl and she deserved having someone dote on her. It was also nice having a female touch around the place.

There is even food in the fridge!

The weather is starting to turn cold. It was 48°F last night. (A summer morning back in Iowa!) The daytime highs, however, have been nice; usually staying in the mid-70s.

The nightlife around town has been okay, I guess. I rarely go out anymore. As of lately, all I've done is work and sleep. I have pretty much stopped seeing any of the girls I used to date. There is no common interest and I just don't have the time.

I can't wait until tomorrow. Tomorrow is the start of my vacation, and at 8 AM I'm off until next week Tuesday. One full week!

I am traveling to Los Angeles to sail on a 'booze cruise' to Ensenada Mexico aboard the USS Azure Seas with my dad, Richard Flewelling, and I can't wait.

But first, I've got to get through today. Things did not go well this morning. When I jumped into the Scout, the battery was dead. Fine! I pulled my Pontiac Fierro out alongside and jump-started the Scout. I then put the Fierro away and jumped into the Scout. The gas tank was empty! So I switched to the reserve tank, which was also empty! I'm now ready to kill my roommate who had borrowed my vehicle leaving it in this shape.

Fortunately, I was able to roll down the hill to the closest gas station. Mind you, I was now late for work. After gassing up, I scooted off to work. Needless to say the supervisors were displeased with me being late.

To keep fueling the fire, I was working with Nancy Martin today out of Unit 87 from substation 9. As usual, business was steady to occasionally heavy. The morning entailed a slew of non-emergency calls; a transfer of 'Aunt Mildred' from Beverly Manor to Valley emergency room to have her hangnail removed and then to take her back. Really exciting stuff! We continued these mind-numbing calls until midday.

Our first challenging call involved a man suffering a severe heart attack. He presented as a textbook heart attack. He was lying in bed, cool, ashen, and extremely sweaty. He was also propped up on a pillow and complaining of a sudden onset of sub-sternal chest pain radiating into his left arm and up to his jaw. He related that the symptoms came on suddenly and while at rest. He also related that he knew he had heart problems and that he took a nitroglycerin tablet under his tongue, but experienced no relief.

When we attached him to the ECG monitor, we saw a normal sinus rhythm with an elevated S-T segment (part of the cardio-electric tracing that corelates well with poor or no blood flow through coronary arteries). We placed him on oxygen and started an IV, then gave him another nitroglycerin tablet and checked his vital signs (pulse, blood pressure, respirations). Although he had taken two nitroglycerin tablets 5 minutes apart he was still experiencing significant chest pain, so we gave him almost 10 mg of morphine to relieve his pain and to dilate his coronary blood vessels. Fortunately, he did not show any premature ventricular contractions (PVCs), so we did not have to start him on lidocaine or give him a 100 mg lidocaine bolus. After a few minutes, the morphine made him feel much better and we placed him on our gurney, loaded him into the ambulance, and monitored him en route to the hospital. Once in the emergency room, he was immediately evaluated and taken to the cardiac catheterization lab for emergency cardiac catheterization with streptokinase. (An emergency procedure in which a catheter is run from the femoral artery up into the heart to dissolve clots in the coronary arteries.)

The rest of the day maintained a steady balance of calls every 1 1/2 hours. At 10:30 PM, we received a call to a fairly affluent part of town. The Fire Department Rescue paramedics had just walked in the front door as we pulled up. Nancy went in first and I followed with the stretcher. As I entered the room, I saw an elderly male patient slumped in a chair, who appeared extremely pale. I heard Nancy tell one of the Fire Department paramedics, "let's get the ECG paddles on him and see if he's got a rhythm." They did and determined that there was none. The ECG demonstrated a course ventricular fibrillation, so we laid him on the floor and started CPR. This was one of those cases where the patient had been in cardiac arrest too long to actually be saved, but not down long enough to call him dead on the scene.

Nancy began to ventilate with an Ambu bag and mask, while the Fire Department medics looked for arm veins to start an IV. While they were doing this, I performed cardiac compressions.

Nancy made two attempts to intubate the patient without any luck, and the Fire Department medics weren't finding any veins. Nancy said, "Ty, I can't get him tubed. You try."

Intubation is a skill that I'm very good at. I switched places with Nancy and inserted laryngoscope blade, and intubating him on my very first attempt. This really embarrassed Nancy, and she began to grumble under her breath. I switched places with Nancy and continued chest compressions while Nancy ventilated the patient and prepared to administer medications down the endotracheal tube.

The Fire Department medics still hadn't started an IV, so I switched places with one of them and as luck would have it, was able to start the line. I then went back to chest compressions. The patient was still in ventricular fibrillation, so we defibrillated him again at 340watt/sec, but he didn't convert. We attempted one last defib, but again, no change in his rhythm.

We then gave an amp of epinephrine down the endotracheal tube and pushed an amp of atropine via his IV line with no change in his rhythm. We again shocked him at 340watt/sec which converted him into an idioventricular rhythm at a rate of 20 bpm.

Since there was no pulse, we continued CPR. We then placed him on the gurney and loaded him into the ambulance. By this time, our patient's rhythm had slipped back into ventricular fibrillation and we couldn't convert him into any salvageable rhythm. We transported him to the hospital and they continued the resuscitation efforts for a while but later pronounced him dead in the emergency room. It was probably for the best. If he would have lived, he would have been brain-dead.

The rest of the shift slowed down a little; a lots of canceled calls and nothing really major. There were a few assault cases as well as a few "man down" calls.

8 AM rolled around and I was off for Los Angeles and my vacation! As I was heading to my car, dispatch was asking if I wanted to work another shift. I just laughed and said, "You want me to do what? Hah, Hah, Hah. You guys are so funny! Hah, hah, hah!"

8 AM Wednesday, 17 October, 1984

I changed clothes, jumped into the Scout and headed for Los Angeles. There were a couple of parties going on around L.A. that Dad and I covered. One was a celebration at the Anheuser-Busch plant in Santa Fe Springs, California, and the other was at a local bar in Chino California called "The Studebaker Lounge." Both were great fun, but the height of my vacation, started Friday afternoon when we boarded the USS Azure Seas.

This kid was ready to have a good time! The food on board was fantastic; the entertainment, first rate; and the women, gorgeous!

Everyone was out to have a good time, and a good time we had! We boarded the ship Friday afternoon and met up with Dad's friends for a glass of champagne. After sharing a toast for a fun and relaxing weekend, we stepped outside to the railing to wave goodbye to the port as the ship set sail.

It looked more like a New Year's Eve party than a ship departing for sea. There were streamers and noisemakers; everyone wore a name tag to make it easier to meet and chat with fellow passengers. As Dad and I looked over the railing, we spotted two attractive ladies that were similar in age to us. My father looked at me and said, "Let me show you how this is done, son." He then took his name tag and stuck it to the end of a streamer and dropped it down to the ladies below. All the while, only making eye contact with me. It wasn't two seconds later that there was a tug on the end of the streamer. My dad smiled with a fake look of surprise and said, "Oh, I think I have a bite!" We looked down and waved to the two ladies looking up at us waving. Since they already knew my father's name (Richard), I was introduced as my father's son, Ty. The ladies were a mother and daughter team, Angela and Heather. We exchanged pleasantries between the floors and suggested that we meet in the bar area after dinner.

I thought I had brought along a big appetite to dinner, but this buffet was beyond belief. I went along the buffet line and took my fair share of everything the chef had to offer. I mean I thoroughly stuffed myself! I couldn't believe that they could serve such a huge amount of food four times a day. After dinner, we rolled ourselves into the upper bar area. We shared a drink with Angela and Heather, who were from the Los Angeles area. Dad seemed to hit it off rather well with Angela, but Heather had her eyes set on someone else at the bar. This did not bother me in the least. I was determined to experience everything this ship had to offer and wasn't interested in spending the rest of the evening making small talk in a bar. I excused myself and went upstairs to watch the entertainment show on the main deck. When the show ended, I strolled downstairs to the lowest level and danced the night away in the ship's disco. When the disco closed at 1 AM, I went back upstairs and closed the casino! During my rampage on the ship, I met several beautiful girls that wanted to either dance, drink, or gamble. So while in the disco I danced with the dancers, then drank with the drinkers, and then closed the casino with the gamblers.

As the girls retired to their cabins, I struck up a conversation with three other guys who were sitting at the same blackjack table. One was a cop from the Los Angeles police department, another was a psychiatrist, and the last was a real estate agent. (Which sounds like the beginning of the joke! "A cop, a psychiatrist, and real estate agent walk into a casino...") We were all highly inebriated, and I had just taken the casino for about $400 before they closed the blackjack table down.

The psychiatrist said, "Come on, I got a bottle of cognac in my cabin." So as the casino kicked us out, and locked the door; we staggered down to the psychiatrist's cabin, and he came out with his bottle of cognac. Apparently his wife was not impressed with his inebriated state. He said, "Well men, might as well make a night of it, I've just been kicked out of my cabin." So we all (four guys and three girls) staggered back up to one of the closed bars. The cop hotwired the jukebox, and the real estate agent jumped behind the bar to discover that the soda and seltzer dispenser was still functional. So we sat, listening to music, drinking cognac, cognac and coke, cognac and tonic or whatever else the dispenser would spit out until sunrise, which came at around 5 AM.

I made my way back to my cabin with the help of "Kathy" (one of the girls I had met earlier) who had decided to help us finish off the evening. Kathy poured me into my cabin and gave me a kiss goodbye.

I awoke at noon to find we had docked in Ensenada, Mexico. I was experiencing an extremely powerful hangover. Three aspirins and a light breakfast later, I disembarked from our ship and worked my way through the Pueblo of Ensenada destined for the famous bar "Hussongs".

Hussongs was an old rickety bar favored by tourists visiting Ensenada. It was an extremely bright and sunny day, and I had forgotten my sunglasses! I swear, the first vendor selling sunglasses could have charged me $1000 and I would have eagerly paid it! The bright light was not helping my hangover, nor were the thousands of vendors trying to get me to buy everything from T-shirts, to sombreros, to hookers. All I wanted to do was get from point A to point B without my head exploding!

Dad and his friends cheered as I entered the bar. I was not in the mood for any more alcohol, but the crowd said "the hair of the dog" was exactly what I needed. A couple beers later, I was almost feeling human again. The group ate lunch and then split up to do a bit of shopping in the little stores that lined the street. I purchased a few small items and then returned to the ship at around 4 PM. Once on board, I again ate more than I should have.

After a two-hour siesta, I again hit all the shows, closed down the disco and bars before going to bed. Sunday morning, I still felt bloated from all the eating I had been doing. So I got up early, and ran three miles around the ship on their exercise track, and then joined an aerobics class. After a vigorous workout, I went up on to the sundeck and fell asleep on a chase recliner in the sun. It was really nice to be able to just relax and let the gentle rocking of the ship unwind all my tension. The sun really felt good with temperatures staying in the low 80s.

On that gentle rocking ship, old memories again bubbled to the surface; events in my childhood, old girlfriends and new ones, things I did with the Woodbury County Sheriff's Department in Iowa, and emergency calls that stuck out in my mind more clearly than others.

One particular call that stood out in my memory took place about two weeks ago on a day that I was working on American Medic 3 with Paul Young. It was the first call of the day. We were relaxing in our substation until 11 AM when we received a call for a possible drowning out at an old golf course. Paul and I jumped into the ambulance and headed off for our destination. The location was out in the sticks and not close to any emergency response assets. Rescue 13 had arrived ahead of us and were performing CPR on a 20-month old girl that had been found by her parents floating face down in a small pond in front of their house. The family related that they were just moving into the house and they thought that their little girl was taking a nap. When she wasn't in her room, they searched around the house, but it was one of her older sisters that found her in the pond. They figured she had been there for about 15 to 20 minutes before being found. The parents knew CPR and immediately started chest compressions and mouth-to-mouth ventilations. Rescue 13 arrived a few minutes later and took over resuscitation efforts.

Upon our arrival, we brought in our advanced life support equipment and began more intensive measures. We suctioned out as much water as we could; intubated the little girl; attached our ECG monitor; and attempted defibrillation at 200 watt/sec. When no change was noted on the monitor, we picked up the little girl and placed her in the back of our ambulance to work under a more controlled setting. The family members were understandably upset and more relatives started showing up as we sat on scene. We established an IV and pushed one half an amp of sodium bicarb and an amp of epinephrine, and again attempted defibrillation at 200watt/sec.

We were extremely pleased when we were able to get a rhythm back with a pulse, but the rate was too slow at 40 beats per minute, in a child whose heart rate should be around 120 bpm. So CPR was continued and an additional .5 mg of atropine was given to increase her heart rate, but to no avail.

We lost her pulse again, but we kept up the chest compressions and ventilation efforts, and then re-bolus with epi and sodium bicarb, but we were unable to regain a pulse. Once at the hospital, resuscitation efforts continued, but the little girl couldn't be saved.

The family members took the news extremely hard. The little girl's parents were taken in to view her body. Once there, they asked to be left alone for a moment. When the nurse returned, she found the parents doing CPR on the little girl. It broke the nurse's heart to see. She called the ER Doc, and hospital chaplain and as a group they gently encouraged the parents to let go.

The little girl had been the youngest of eight in the family. The family was musically oriented, sort of like the Osmond family.

Calls, like that one, are hard to forget. Luckily, they don't happen that often.

The sun was starting to become overcast, so I grabbed my tanning oil and went inside to see what everyone else was up to. I found Dad with his friends up in the Miramar lounge. They all looked like they had had a pretty rough night last night. We went down to the dining hall and ate, and then went back upstairs to watch the evening's entertainment. My first cruise was coming to an end and I had a fantastic time. Hopefully, I'll be able to do it again next year.

The next morning came quickly and before I knew it, I was saying goodbye to everyone I had met. I hugged my Dad and headed back for Las Vegas. I arrived back to my house at around 4 PM, and amazingly found what I thought were my ex-roommates, still living in the house.

I had just gotten back from vacation, and already my nerves were starting to fray. The worst was yet to come. Seems the bank had lost my payroll check and the computer had my account all screwed up. So my bank statement appeared as if I only had $100 in my checking account instead of $1000. This meant my rent check would bounce when it hit the bank.

Work was also in turmoil. While I was away, an ambulance had been broadsided and in a separate event, the Mercy Senior Executive, Bob Forbus, had been arrested on drunk driving charges and was all over the news. I went home and hid!

I tell you! Leave the company alone for one week and it falls apart! Unbelievable!

8 AM Tuesday, 22 October, 1984

I'm working with Paul Young again today. Rumor has it that I'm going to be placed on American full-time and that Paul is going to be my regular partner. From the looks of my upcoming schedule, I'd say the rumors were correct. I'm back on my regular Tuesday, Thursday, Sunday schedule on American with Paul as my partner. I am thrilled. I like working on the American ambulances, which are a lot more stable. I'll always have the same substation, work with the same people, and the same Fire Department personnel.

The shift started smoothly; we had an elderly man that awoke to discover he couldn't move his entire left side. It was very sad. He lived alone and had no relatives or close friends to look in on him. He said that it took him 2 ½ hours just to get to the phone to call for help. He also told us that he had tried to get the attention of his neighbors by yelling, but no one stopped to investigate.

It is not uncommon that when a person is having a stroke, like in this gentleman's case, they'll also have cardiac issues. Our patient was experiencing a lot of irregular heartbeats. This can happen when the part of the brain that controls certain heart function is affected. Our man was extremely sick. I started an IV and gave him a bolus of 100 mg lidocaine to suppress the ectopic beats that were present on his ECG.

Our patient's name was John, and a real nice guy. John explained to me that he was an independent type of person and had been taking care of himself since his wife died in 1979. Sadly, John's days of taking care of himself were over. John had suffered a massive stroke and was completely paralyzed on the left side of his body, leaving John no choice but to move into a nursing home where he could receive appropriate care.

While writing up the report at the hospital, I couldn't help but think a move like that would probably be the end of John. He was an extremely spirited individual, whose body had just given out. A life having to sit in a nursing home and wait for someone else to help him do everything would probably be too much. After dropping John off at Valley hospital, we proceeded to Station 1 to re-supply our ambulance.

Activity around Station 1 was quiet, which was a nice change. We grabbed what we needed and headed for our section of town. Paul had a few errands to run, so we buzzed around our area getting his errands out of the way. Paul's Toyota pickup had been acting up, so he took it down to the local dealer to have it worked on.

The day was very pleasant; blue sky; warm weather, and not really that busy. Early in the afternoon, we received a call for an automobile accident. It appeared that a man in an old beat up Dodge pickup broadsided a man in a brand-new Porsche, totaling the car. No one was physically injured, but the owner of the Porsche was crying so hysterically that the police thought they'd better call us just to check him out. We arrived on-scene and tried to find out what was bothering him, all he did say was, "I only had 200 miles on it." Then he'd start bawling again. We didn't transport him anywhere, I just told him, "Go home and rest, you've had a pretty hard day and shouldn't overdo it."

Just after we cleared the scene of this accident, we received a call for a man bitten by a dog. As we went en route, I envisioned some poor man having a German Shepherd gnaw on his arm or leg with flesh and blood everywhere.

We arrived on scene, and discovered that a disagreement had arisen between a taxicab driver, and the dog's owner. The dog in question looked like an aged "speedy" from the TV show "Little Rascals". (You know the white dog with a black patch over one eye.) The person bitten was the cab driver, who had a couple scratches and what looked like maybe one tooth mark. I wasn't even sure it was actually a dog bite.

The Metro Police Department had arrived and was trying to settle the dispute. I walked over to the vicious canine in question, who was sitting near-by quietly wagging his tail. I knelt down beside him and started petting his head. He looked up and started licking my hand. I looked over to the cab driver and the police officers and asked, "Is this the dog that bit you?" The cabbie said, "Yes!" I said, "He doesn't look so fierce to me, what did you do to irritate him?" He said, "Nothing! All I did was pull the old man out of my cab." I said, "What did you expect would happen, when you manhandle the dog's master?" I looked over at Paul, who was shaking his head. Paul said,

"Come on, this guy can find his own way to the hospital."

We stayed busy the rest of the day; a couple seizures; a broken hip; and a woman that supposedly overdosed on heroin. She was a real beaut!

When we arrived on that scene, we were met by her boyfriend, who told us he had tried to get her to go with him to the hospital, but she wouldn't. He asked if we could do something with her. As we walked into the apartment, we were met by sailing pots and pans and obscene language. Paul blew up. He kicked open the door and ran into the apartment dodging pots and pans, and grabbed the supposedly overdosing girl by her hair and threw her against the wall. Paul said, "Now you listen to me you little cunt! We risked our lives racing across town to help you and you greet us with obscene language and violence! You know people like you deserve what you get or do to yourself. I'll be damned if I'll transport you in my ambulance!" With that he threw her onto the bed.

I had just stepped into the room by then and asked her, "Did you take any pills or shoot up today?" She looked up at me and said, "Fuck you!" I stood there looking at her in a non-committal fashion and said, "That ain't gonna happen" and followed Paul out the door.

As we were walking to our ambulance, the girl's boyfriend came running over to us yelling, "Hey! What am I supposed to do?" Paul turned around and said in a very calm and straight-forward voice, "Move." We then started the ambulance and headed back to our substation.

We received calls intermittently for the rest of the night. As usual, our final call was received at 7:45 AM just 15 minutes before shift was to end. I don't know why this happened. The dispatchers know that we are to get off at 8 AM, but they still seem to manage to find calls for us to run on a regular basis just before shift change.

Just prior to shift change, Paul and I were at Desert Springs hospital picking up Paul's girlfriend's car for Paul to drive home at the end of the shift. We were about three blocks away from the substation when the call came in. So I just drove to the substation and was going to have Paul jump in with me to run the call.

It happened that both of the relieving crew members were already there, so they decided to run the call, which Paul and I thought was great! Paul had to be in class in an hour and I sure didn't mind getting off on time, for a change. Unfortunately, my supervisor didn't feel the same way. Boy, did I get in trouble! It was explained to me in less than ten brief sentences that when I received a call, I run it. Period!

Their anger didn't last very long though. The company knows who is reliable and who isn't. They tried very hard to keep me happy. If they didn't, ... Well suddenly I'm really busy and can't fill in at a moment's notice.

8 AM Wednesday, 23 October, 1984

I went home and relaxed until around noon. Bob and Shelley were both working, so I had the house to myself. Dr. Guy Posey (ER Doc) and Bob Dean (Paramedic), friends from the EMS system back home in Iowa, were in Las Vegas on vacation and had been riding along with some of the EMS crews checking out our system. I rang them up and asked them to stop by. They managed to swing by the house that evening.

It was great fun going down memory lane, talking about the old days with Midwest Inner-city ambulance, the old civil defense teams, Sheriff's rescue squad calls, and emergency department work. They were all good memories, but like all memories, that is where they must remain. As nice as it was to talk to Bob and Guy, I knew I could never return to that EMS system. It just would never work. I truly think it would kill me. I made a vow to myself that as long as I could help it, I'd never take a step backwards, and that I would always try and steadily progress forward and upward both personally and professionally.

6 – END OF THE YEAR PUSH

November, 1984

Bob had told me that they were unsure if they were going to move in with Robin Nunn or not. I said, "Well, Robin believes you two are moving in for sure." Shelley said, "Well I just don't know her that well and all." I replied, "Robin's good people." Shelly continued to hem and haw on with indecision, but I turned a deaf ear to it, thinking about the fact that they had been in the house an extra month without paying rent and not only was I taking it in the shorts, so was Robin. I was positive she had budgeted everything around them moving in with her.

Robin Nunn and I decided that we had had it with roommates leaving us in limbo and hung out to dry. Bob and Shelley had been telling everyone that they were intending to move out on me, every one that is, but me! They had told Robin that they were going to move in with her, but then backed out at the last minute putting Robin in a major financial jam. Jim Cox still hadn't paid me for his final month's rent, and Bob only paid me half of what he owed me. My charitability had completely dried up. I decided that everything I did would have a price tag on it, and if you couldn't afford the price or if I couldn't get something in return out of it, tough! Find someone else.

So Robin and I sat down and figured out our own game plan, which was for Robin to move in with me. I went home and told Bob that Robin was moving in to my place next Saturday and that he would have to find his own place. Saturday rolled around, but Bob still hadn't moved. Robin hadn't disassembled her waterbed yet and was spending the last night at her house before moving to my place on Xavier street. I sat down with Bob and once again explained that, if he didn't notice, Robin was moving in and he would be completely moved out by tomorrow and that all his stuff would have to be out in the front yard. Bob said he understood. He had an ambulance standby event to go to in the morning, but that he would definitely get things going in the afternoon. I said that that was fine with me. Bob and Shelley were in and out all day, but by 6 PM nothing had been moved. I was pissed. "Robin," I said, "get me some boxes. Bob is moving now!" I had three quarters of Bob's stuff boxed and sitting out on the back patio when he came home. He ranted and raved for a while but I didn't care. What I said stood. I said, "I'll be nice to you Bob. I'll let you sleep on the couch if you want, but you don't get to live here anymore. Which reminds me, I would like the keys to my house, car, and truck back." Bob started into the old "some friend you are" routine. I came back with "Don't give me that bullshit Bob, who was it that let you use my car and truck free of charge and had both vehicles returned to me emptied of gas more than once, by you? Who was it that covered you for two weeks until you could make rent payments? Who was it that said they were going to move in with Robin but then backed out the day they said they were moving in, which left her high and dry? Who, Bob?!!! So don't give me this 'some friend' bullshit. You have worn that friendship out. Like I said, if you want, you can sleep on the couch tonight, but you don't live here anymore." He mumbled some more but nothing was said. Later on, when we were out of Bob's earshot, Robin said to me, "Just wait until the rumor mill starts up at work." I replied, "You don't have to worry about that. Bob knows better. He knows it would do him a lot more harm to say something bad about me. I have too many friends and influence." And just as I predicted, nothing was said.

Between the stuff that Robin owns and the stuff that I have, the house looks pretty nice! Robin is a friend. She is seven or eight years older than I am, divorced with a teenage daughter that lives with her father in Wyoming. While we get along great, we are just platonic roommates. Nothing romantic.

As far as girlfriends go, I've pretty much given up even looking. It seems like every time I start going out with someone, they seem to take everything that I do for them for granted. I don't know, it just seems to me that if someone were to take me to an expensive (or maybe not expensive) but real nice restaurants, I would try to be courteous and thankful; not just tell their friends about all the expensive places their date took me, or what they were going to expect next. Does this make any sense? It is about equal support of the relationship.

Maybe if I gave an example: there are many really nice relatively inexpensive restaurants in town, with an excellent menu, superb atmosphere and music even though they may not appear all that elegant from the outside. Then there are other places that have neither elegance nor class, but have outrageous prices on their menus. It seemed that the girls I've taken out would rather go to a place that requires you to spend big bucks for the evening, but provides nothing as far as good entertainment or atmosphere, rather than to a place that is inexpensive, but entertaining.

There had been a few girls that I had taken out that I was sure couldn't tell the difference between the "Top of the Mint" and "McDonald's." It had been very discouraging to my Iowa Farm boy sensibilities. So as it stood, I would wrap myself up in my work and worry about a relationship at a later date. But don't worry about me stepping completely out of circulation. I have enough friends that like to use me as a wing-man on their blind dates.

Work, as usual was the high point and most exciting part of my life. I had become more and more involved with the public relations portion of Mercy ambulance. In January 1985, I would start the revised drinking and driving lectures at local high schools and would assist Mercy ambulance in starting a junior paramedic group for high schoolers between the ages of 14 and 20. The group is sponsored by the Boy Scouts of America and I will be their advisor. Mercy indicated that they are going to help me hire a professional videographer to film my drunk driving lectures. Exciting stuff. I'm also developing a few small projects that I hope to sell.

Last week was the American Ambulance Association Convention. It was held in the Las Vegas Convention Center and pulled Ambulance Services from all across the nation. I managed to attend four days of the week-long event. I introduced myself to several ambulance service managers across the nation. Major owners such as Chuck Braun of Braun Ambulances, Steve Athey of Medevac Mid-America, Dave Williams of Horton Ambulance Service in San Diego California, Mr. Schaffer of Schaffer Ambulance Service Southern California, and others from Milwaukee to Miami, and New York to Portland. They now knew my name. At one time I was worried that I had all my eggs in one basket. Not anymore. While Mercy ambulance would never fire me, it was good to have options, if I were to ever quit. I could have had a new job in a week almost anywhere in the US.

As one ambulance company owner related to me, "Paramedics are becoming a dime a dozen, but only a rough 1000 paramedics really know what it is all about. If you have a couple of those 1000 medics working for you, it can make a big difference in how your entire service operates. Look me up when you're tired of Mercy."

The Thanksgiving weekend was extremely busy. Most of the ambulances in town were transporting 15 to 20 patients per shift. I had been scheduled to work Wednesday, Thursday and Saturday to cover those on vacation. In actuality, I worked a 12 hour shift on Monday, I was on-call on Tuesday and was pulled in for 6 hours, a 24 hour shift on Wednesday, a 24 hour shift on Thursday, and an 8 hour office day on Friday, followed by another 24 hour shift on Saturday. Sunday I slept in!

After waking up on Sunday afternoon, I relaxed around the house. The weather had started to cool off with daytime highs in the mid-50s and evening lows in the low 30s. Thanksgiving week was also rainy and misty, leaving the streets extremely greasy and resulting in a tenfold increase in automobile accidents. Sadly, many people were killed on the streets and highways in and around Las Vegas.

Robin's boyfriend is an investigator for the coroner's office, so I get to hear about the follow-up on fatalities that I respond to, as well as other deaths in the Valley. One particular case happened near Mount Charleston, about two miles away from the crash I had responded to earlier in the year in Kyle Canyon. He related that two couples had been up at the Mount Charleston Lodge partying and having a real crazy time. They were on their way back down the mountain when their car stalled. The two guys were out trying to flag down a ride back into town. It was pitch black out, both men were wearing dark clothing and had dark hair, a recipe for disaster. Traffic couldn't see them and weren't stopping. Being extremely intoxicated (their blood alcohol levels were over .30, where .10 is legally drunk), the men were getting upset that traffic wasn't stopping. When the next vehicle came by, they jumped in front of it. The first guy took most of the impact from the pickup into his shoulder and was thrown out into the desert. He landed on a large boulder, breaking his neck and was killed instantly. The second man was grazed by the side of the truck, but was hit by the streamline trailer-home that the truck was pulling. The impact was so hard that the guy literally exploded, sending chunks of flesh, blood, and brain matter flying over the men's wives who were standing by their stalled car. While both men were pronounced dead at the scene, their wives were taken to the hospital for treatment of hysteria.

Monday, 19 November, 1984

I was on-call for Mercy ambulance and carrying the back-up beeper. While I stayed close to the house, there was stuff I needed to get done. One can't just hang by the phone waiting to be called in. There was yard work to do! It was almost to be expected that after putting a long hard day's work trimming trees, draining the pool, raking the yard and picking up garbage, that Mercy would call me into work. I was just stepping out of the shower as they called so I put on the uniform and headed for Station 1.

I felt exhausted as I worked the rest of the evening. To make matters worse, all we did was cover other Unit areas while they were en route to the hospital. They finally let me go home at 2 AM.

Oh, we did run one call. It was at the Boulevard Mall. The call came in as a "woman down", just at closing time. It turned out that the woman in question had been caught shoplifting and suddenly became mysteriously ill. I walked up to her and asked, "What's wrong?" She moaned and mumbled something. I said, "What? I can't hear you. How can I help you when you won't tell me what's wrong?" She said, "I'm sick." I replied, "That's like telling me it's dark out. It doesn't tell me much." What's wrong with you?" She rolled around on the floor a little bit then said, "My stomach hurts." I knelt down on the floor by her, took my penlight and looked at her eyes, which were constricted, I then felt her pulse, which was beating rapidly, I looked at her, took a deep breath inside. "Okay, enough with the games. What are you on? Speed? Coke? Greens? What." She looked at me with a sort of surprised look and said, "Honest. I'm not on nothing. I usually take some Valiums, but not tonight." I said, "Right, you're lying to me, girl. As far as I'm concerned you're healthy enough to go to jail and if I have to run on you again you will wish you WERE ill. Book'em Danno."

I explained to the security guards that there was nothing wrong with her and to watch her because given the right opportunity, I was sure that she would try and take off. We went 10-8 (back in service) and continued to cover other Units.

Tuesday, 20 November, 1984

Tuesday, I slept in until noon and then finished the remaining errands and yard work around the house. That evening, I was asked to work ambulance stand-by at a very prestigious event (so I was told). The event was Casino owner, Benny Binion's 80th birthday party. Corey Friedman, Mercy Paramedic was working the event with me. We met one of the owners of Mercy ambulance (Mr. Bell) at 7 PM out alongside the building in which the festivities were to take place. Mr. Bell met us in the parking lot of an ARCO gas station, which adjoined the banquet hall. He said, "You guys just sit here. If I need you, I'll send the maître d' out for you."

FIVE DAMN HOURS Corey and I sat in that parking. They wouldn't let us come in, nor did they send any food out to us. We finally went over to the gas station and ordered food to be delivered to the ambulance. I'll bet it was the most unusual delivery that guy had ever delivered. I asked Corey after he hung up the phone "Well? Did they believe you?" Corey shrugged his shoulders and said, "Well, we will find out." The delivery guy showed up without any problems and the rest of the evening Corey entertained me with card tricks and slight-of-hand magic. Corey was an amateur magician and comedian and had hoped to be able to entertain the crowd this evening and perhaps get a paid gig. I would have hired him! He really was quite amazing!

THEN, the straw that broke the camel's back! That jerk, Bell, forgot all about us and didn't bother to tell us when the party was over. I was so pissed. I told dispatch that the next time Mr. Bell wanted an ambulance for a standby, he'd better not call me because I'd tell him what he could do with his standbys. A couple of days later, Bob

Forbus, (Executive Manager of Mercy) stopped by to apologize for what had happened. I would have preferred an apology directly from Mr. Bell himself, but that wasn't going to happen.

7 AM Wednesday, 21 November, 1984

I started a 24-hour shift at the downtown substation. It was still raining and calls were stacked up in dispatch. Every time an ambulance cleared from one call, another call was waiting. I was really getting behind on my paperwork. Transporting one patient at a time isn't bad, but when you start taking two or three in one shot, it's almost impossible to keep up with the documentation.

One call involved a couple that were hit head-on by a drunk driver. The husband was a painter by trade and had several five gallon buckets of paint in the van with them. When they were struck, their van rolled and was not only completely totaled but the interior (and its occupants) were completely covered in enamel paint! Both husband and wife were severely injured, and both were completely drenched in enamel based paint! They had paint in their eyes; paint in their mouths and in their ears, and their hair was completely matted down with enamel paint. We had to completely cover everything in the ambulance so as not to get paint on everything. I completely trashed out my uniform. It was like tar and feathers. You couldn't clean up their lacerations or appropriately splint and dress anything. I didn't care for the drunk in the other vehicle, but apparently he died later in the hospital.

The evening and night continued non-stop. That night, we responded to a house fire where five people were supposedly trapped inside. We arrived on-scene and anxiously awaited near the house in the pouring rain for the firefighters to knock down the flames and determine if there truly was anyone in the house or at least anyone left that could still be saved.

After being completely drenched by the rain, the Fire Department decided there wasn't anyone in the house. We dragged our sniffley, coughing, aching cold bodies back into our ambulance and headed back towards our substation only to be given another call. I sincerely didn't believe I was going to be able to finish that shift. We had to fill up with gas twice and ran out of invoices once.

Then I remembered, I have to work another 24-hour shift tomorrow. I thought to myself, *There's no way I could do it. Not after last night*

7 AM Thursday, 22 November, 1984

I stepped out of one ambulance and climbed into another. We went back to the substation, where I called dispatch and told them that I needed 45 minutes to get cleaned up for my next shift. In that 45 minutes, they spared us from three calls.

We started in again. Luckily, I had a neonatal transfer at noon and had a three hour layover between our arrival and the return trip. Those three hours of sleep were a Godsend. I was grateful for the rest. Upon returning to service after the transfer, we didn't slow down until 7 PM. We finally were allowed to eat the cold Thanksgiving dinner that had been held at Mercy ambulance Station 1 five hours before. But the food was still good and our hungry appetites wasted no time digging in. We had just finishing dessert, when we were called back into service.

The call was for a "man down", which turned out to be a long distance from Station 1. John Graff and I jumped into the ambulance and headed across town to Sam's Town Casino and Resort. I said to John, "I can't believe that there wasn't a closer Unit." John responded, "It's going to be a code (cardiac arrest). I can feel it. Anytime I have to travel a super long distance, where my response time looks horrible, the patient is always critical."

We arrived at Sam's Town 20 minutes later and I looked through the front glass store windows to see the Fire Department engine company doing CPR. I gave a heavy sigh and said, "John it's a code." John just said, "It figures." We went in with our equipment and started to work.

The patient was a 62-year-old man from Omaha, Nebraska. He had been in town a couple of days. His wife related that he had complained earlier in the day of chest pains, but told her it was nothing and not to be worried. He had a past history of heart attacks and was on an extensive list of medications. When he collapsed, he vomited and aspirated vomit into his lungs. He was also incontinent of urine and fecal matter. We hooked him up to the cardiac monitor, which showed ventricular fibrillation.

We shocked him twice but had no change in his cardiac rhythm. CPR was continued. I started an IV and gave two Amps of sodium bicarbonate and an amp of epinephrine. His ECG went to flatline (asystole). We gave him an amp of atropine and hooked him up to an Isuprel drip.

Shortly thereafter, we noticed the return of a pulse and his ECG demonstrated a super ventricular rhythm at a rate of 140 bpm. I started the second IV and hooked up a dopamine drip. His heartbeat was good and strong, so we turned down the Isuprel and turned up the dopamine. His blood pressure stabilized at 60/40, but he still wasn't making respiratory effort on his own. We placed him on our gurney and went en route to Desert Springs hospital. When we left him at the hospital, he was about ready to be transported to the intensive care Unit. didn't know how long he'd last. He had been down for about 17 minutes prior to our arrival with only basic CPR. Ideally, an ACLS ambulance should arrive on scene within eight minutes to affect a positive outcome. Additionally, aspirating a full stomach into his lungs didn't help.

Time would tell, I guess.

The rest of the day maintained a steady pace. By the time 12 hours of my second shift had passed, I was dead tired, grumpy, and working on a mega cold. The worst thing was that my patient care was starting to deteriorate. In the past 36 hours, I had taken care of 20 critical patients and I just couldn't keep my head clear. I was forgetting to pick up equipment and was running on "impulse power" (which is what I call memory motion). Somehow, I managed to make it through the 24 hour shift. I can't tell you about the rest of the calls I had because frankly, I can't remember them.

8 AM Friday, 23 November, 1984

I went home and slept until 4 PM. Robin's boyfriend (Scott) came to the house and fixed his famous spaghetti dinner. We then relaxed and watched TV, sitting by the fireplace. I went back to bed at around 11 PM. I had to work in the morning and I didn't want to be worn out if I had another bad shift.

8 AM Saturday, 24 November, 1984

Work started off with the usual finesse. I was working with Rick Cozad, a paramedic that I had never worked with before. Rich had a reputation as a know-it-all paramedic. But needed to keep his mouth shut and his eyes and ears open. A dozen medics from the company had refused to work with him. With such a street reputation, I was slightly tense about working with him.

The day started off without any problems. Rick had a good sense of humor and for the greater part of the day, we just talked about things in general. He was a guitarist and actually looked a little like Steven Ray Von. None of the calls we ran on were all that challenging and everyone was happy. Later on in the afternoon, our call volume started to pick up. I noticed that Rick's attitude was also starting to change. I couldn't believe it. He started treating patients shitty, mouthing off to me, and acting real arrogant in the emergency departments. It was really starting to get ridiculous.

After dropping off the next patient, I said, "Rick, something's got to change. During the past few calls you have been really nasty to the patients and ignoring the guys on Rescue is going to get you into a lot of hot water fast." Rick just shrugged off what I said, but things did improve on the next call. As the hours wore on, his work started to slow down. It took him forever to get his paperwork done and he was constantly jabbering with the ER staff and forgetting to restock the ambulance.

At 3 AM, all I wanted to do was drop off my patient at the hospital, restock and go back to the substation to sleep. Rick, on the other hand, would rather sit down with the doc and discuss pros and cons of calcium chloride or whatever. It literally took starting to pull away in the ambulance by myself for him to realize I was ready to leave. This shift was really becoming a pain in the ass. I was so glad when 8 AM rolled around and it came to an end. Maybe in time, with a partner that is willing to work with Rick, he could become an excellent paramedic. But the first thing he's got to do is get rid of his attitude problem.

I drove home Sunday and slept until noon. I then cleaned the house, did laundry, and worked on my drinking and driving lecture. I then watched a VCR movie.

Man! It seems like when you get off work, you don't feel like doing anything. Something definitely has to be done about the torturous 24 hour shifts!

Midnight 4 December, 1984

It had been quite an interesting year. Our ambulance statistics show that the average paramedic working full-time for Mercy ambulance transported around 1500 patients and responded to over 3000 calls for help. If you figure there are 40 full-time paramedics divided by 2, it comes to 60,000 calls this year. No wonder paramedic burnout is so high.

My employee number is #163. Employee numbers are above 200 now. Only three paramedics that started under the reorganization of Mercy in 1980 are left and rumor has it that two are leaving next year. Mercy ambulance has a reputation as being one of the busiest ambulance services in the nation. Looking back over the year, I know why. There have been a lot of good and bad things to account for in this past year. Some of the good things:

> I was elated last December to be hired by Mercy ambulance. It represented new hopes, new goals to conquer and the opportunity to work for a much larger ambulance service than what I had been used to working for.
>
> There was the new scenery. New things to do. I now had mountains to climb, deserts to explore, and a large lake to swim and fish.
>
> I had a new town to build a reputation in; as not just an ordinary paramedic, but the best!
>
> It was once said to me that achievements are accomplished by 10% inspiration and 90% perspiration. I think that the perspiration I have put into this job is greater than 90%! That being said, I still have a burning desire to improve and it will always egg me on to be just a little bit better.
>
> I've met a lot of new friends and found out who truly were friends among my old ones.
>
> I am grateful for this job, and for this town. It has made me a better paramedic and has sharpened my skills. Through this life experience I had become more self-confident.

The town itself has spoiled me by being open 24 hours a day. If I wanted to go shopping at 3 AM, I went shopping. Bars never closed and entertainment was around the clock.

On the downside, the girls had really been a big disappointment. I had yet to find one that I clicked with. There were a lot of pretty faces out there, but none that were right for me. I'd met nice girls in Los Angeles, but L.A. is a long way to go for a date!

It had been difficult getting used to not being able to drive the 30 or so miles from Sioux City, Iowa to the comforts of the family farm, and even though I had a bad reputation for disappearing for months at a time, it was nice knowing the family was close by. Now it seemed like I was halfway around the world and the family had been reduced to phone calls and photographs. It was a slight consolation knowing that my cousins, the Elsers' are only a short eight hour drive away, but finding time to get to Fresno for a visit was also fleeting.

I was also deeply grateful for the opportunity to become re-acquainted with my biological father, Richard Flewelling, who lived only four hours away in Chino, California. There is an extraordinary connection between the two of us and I consider our time together priceless. All these family connections helped, but it just wasn't like the old days, when a 45 minute drive was all it took to be able to sit down at the kitchen table and talk.

I was really sorry I wouldn't make it back for Christmas, but as usual I was working. If I'm lucky, I might make it back in the spring. Money was tight and next to impossible to splurge on a surprise plane ticket.

Another item that was hard to swallow was the fact that even though my weekly salary has increased by $100, paramedics were grossly underpaid. For instance, when I delivered a baby, the company would charge $15 for the OB kit, but nothing for me delivering the baby. A doctor would get $1500 for the babies, just like the ones I delivered. If I intubated someone, Mercy charged for the tube; a doctor would've charged $800! The list went on and on and it got a bit discouraging.

The hours that we worked were long and hard and the only reason we made a decent wage was due to the huge number of hours packed into a week. Retirement benefits were a disaster. Basically, no one had worked long enough as a paramedic to retire. This is typically due to injury. Robin, my roommate, just injured her back again. This was the second time in a year. Most likely she would not be returning to the field. Another paramedic in the company just underwent back surgery due to this job.

Although the negatives were few, they were significant. I loved the work that I was doing, but I knew already that I needed to advance my education. I would probably be a paramedic for a few more years; long enough to go back to school and continue my medical career. I was seriously looking at going to medical school to become an M.D., but I had decided I'd rather go to Physician Assistant school. Don Smutzer was the PA that cared for my parents and I while growing up, and if I can become half the "Doctor" he was, I'd consider myself a success.

I hadn't given up on Las Vegas just yet. I had a lot of little projects that I was working on to build the image of the paramedic. In January, my drunk driving lectures would be in full swing and hopefully taped and put on the market.

I was working in conjunction with the Boy Scouts of America and starting the Paramedic Explore program for youth that were interested in the field of prehospital care.

I had invented a couple of small items to be used by paramedics and I hoped to market them next year. By the time I left Las Vegas, I wanted people to know that I had been there.

So in closing, my year-end thoughts, it's been a good year. I've learned a lot and I've seen a lot. Paramedics don't live the same life that other people do. We can't. It's sort of like the guy that comes back from Vietnam. He's not the same as when he went over. What he has seen and what he's done changes him. He sees things through a different lens. The realities of life in the bigger world, outside of his small town bubble changed him. In time he can readjust, but the experiences are still be there.

Paramedics are a lot like that. We see so much. Let's face it, my job is someone else's emergency. This year alone, I've witnessed car wrecks, watched people die in my hands, seen knifings and shootings, taken care of abused women and children, rape victims, heart attacks, strokes and burn victims. The list of emergencies is long.

I felt I had seen it all and then multiple variations of those events. To most paramedics, it's routine. They don't care who it is or what the reason is for the call, the patient gets taken care of.

Whether it's for medical treatments or a little public education, the one thing that we all agree on is that we don't get enough recognition for the extraordinary service we perform in the shadows. I've grown up a lot this year. I'm not as naïve as I was in Iowa. Hopefully it will keep me from making a few mistakes. Hopefully it will make me a better person.

To all of you back in Iowa or wherever you may be, take care this Christmas and propose a toast to me for I will be doing the same for you as I sit in my Jacuzzi in the backyard with new friends that I have met here in Las Vegas and as you shovel all that snow this winter and scurry around through the cold trying to keep from slipping on the ice, just remember one thing... I'M NOT!!!!!

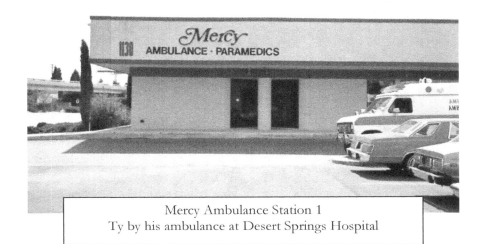

Mercy Ambulance Station 1
Ty by his ambulance at Desert Springs Hospital

MERCY PLAZA BUILDING I
1130 SO. HIGHLAND DRIVE
LAS VEGAS, NEVADA 89102

"People Who Care"

Ty lecturing at a Boulder City High School
Ty on-scene with a Paramedic student Jack Weiss

Ty with Ron Barnes the day he delivered his own son.

PERSONAL TRAGEDY INSPIRES DRIVER SAFETY LECTURES

Mercy Paramedic, Ty Klingensmith, ends his Driver Safety Lecture that focuses on the dangers of Drunk Driving with an account of a personal experience that sobers even the most cavalier high school student at lecture presentations. Sponsored by Mercy Ambulance, it is offered to all local high schools' Driver Education and Health Classes.

At the age of 18, Mr. Klingensmith was the passenger in a motor vehicle accident that occurred at high speeds and resulted in serious injury to himself while his intoxicated friend, the driver, escaped injury.

The Lecture Series presents the realities of a drunk driving incident; the kinematics of a traumatic injury, legal and insurance ramifications, as well as the medical procedures involved for trauma victims.

The lecture combines the use of slides and information compiled by the Department of Transportation and the National Highway and Traffic Safety Department.

Mr. Klingensmith has worked as a Paramedic with Mercy Ambulance for over a year. Before coming to Mercy he worked for the Emergency Services Department in Woodbury County, Iowa as their Training Coordinator.

Ty states he feels his lesson can benefit young drivers and will be offering this presentation throughout the remainder of the school year.

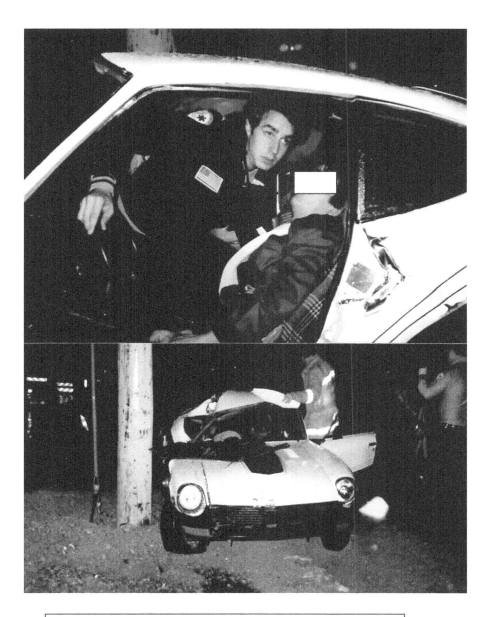

Car versus pole motor vehicle accident

7 - NEW YEAR

16 February, 1985

The days have turned into weeks, and the weeks into months since the last time I sat down to write. So here I sit on a warm evening in February, sipping a favorite cup of hot tea, wondering where the time had gone. It seems like only yesterday I was still looking for Christmas presents!

1984 departed with its usual splendor. Last New Year's Eve (1983), I had to work. In fact, I really can't remember when I had a New Year's Eve off last. I decided this year (1984), I was going to go downtown and witness a world-class Las Vegas New Year's Eve bash firsthand. The weather was brisk but not unbearable, and as the party began with thousands of people gathering, it became quite warm.

The downtown, Fremont street area, had been blocked off from the Union Plaza Hotel and Casino to just past the El Cortez Casino and an additional block on either side. This entire 3 x 5 block area was packed with New Year's Eve partygoers. There were live bands playing on each end of Fremont Street, plus the event was being nationally televised. An event definitely worth witnessing in person!

All the casinos were full, but I managed to slip into a "21" table for a few quick hands of Blackjack. I won $50, so I decided to quit while I was ahead.

The fireworks above the Union Plaza were just starting as I walked outside. The display was spectacular! Like none I had ever seen. They endlessly lit up the sky with one explosion after another.

I had gone downtown alone and although I did run into a few people I knew, I was still basically flying solo. At around 10 PM, I was standing at one end of Fremont Street listening to a jazz band when I met Debbie and Lisa. Debbie was from Kentucky and Lisa was from California. They had come to Vegas for the party but didn't know anyone in town or that much about the city. Naturally, being the public servant that I am, I offered my services to guide them around town. How could they refuse or even resist.

I gave them a guided tour of the downtown area and took them to a few places I knew would really be partying hard. After the New Year's fireworks and champagne Debbie had to catch a flight back to Kentucky at 1:30 in the morning. Lisa and I took her to the airport and saw her off. After dropping Debbie off at the airport, Lisa and I hit a few more parties before driving back to my place to sleep at 4 AM.

At 7 AM, I was up and ready for work. I dropped Lisa off at the airport and headed for the American Ambulance substation. Even though I had been up almost all night, I didn't feel that bad. 1985 had started off with a bang! Unfortunately, it also began with a crunch.

I arrived to work at 8 AM. My partner this New Year's day was Pete's Vier, a part-time American paramedic that usually worked full-time at Mercy. The shift was exceptionally hectic. We headed off on our first call at 8:15 AM and didn't see the substation for the rest of the day.

The calls were basically those to be expected during a hectic holiday timeframe; a couple of overdoses due to holiday depression syndrome, and a few heart attacks from people overdoing it at family gatherings.

Then at 3:30 PM, it happened. Pete and I had been trying to get something to eat all day long and had just stopped at a supermarket near our substation in an attempt to quickly buy some food. We had no sooner turned off the engine when we received another call for a woman that had collapsed at the Tropicana hotel. With a heavy sigh, I started the engine, turned on the emergency lights, and pulled out onto the street with the siren wailing. Pete had just finished writing down the call information from dispatch and had radioed that we were en route when he dropped the mic. I had glanced down at Pete fumbling for the mic on the floor, a mere half a second, but that spit second in a moving vehicle is a lot.

Before glancing down, the car in front of me had signaled their intent to pull to the right, but in that split second had swerved back in front of me and slammed on their brakes. There was nothing I could do. The car was too close. I hit my brakes, then turned hard to the left and the center lane. I was not fast enough. My right front quarter panel and bumper caught the rear end of the stopped car and spun it 360°. We bent our bumper, broke the headlight, crunched the front quarter panel, and flattened the tire. Ambulances are built more like trucks than cars. My damage was mild. The car on the other hand was completely totaled! I'm so grateful that there was only a single female driver in the vehicle, since I put her trunk into her back seat.

I immediately reported the accident to dispatch, confirmed that Pete was okay, then rushed to the car to make sure the lady was okay. Thankfully she was fine, but kept saying, "I stopped so that you could go around me." I sighed and said "Thank you, but you're supposed to pull to the right and then stop."

She was cited for failure to yield to an emergency vehicle and since I struck her from the rear, I was also cited for "due care with accident", which was later dropped to "illegal parking", a non-moving violation.

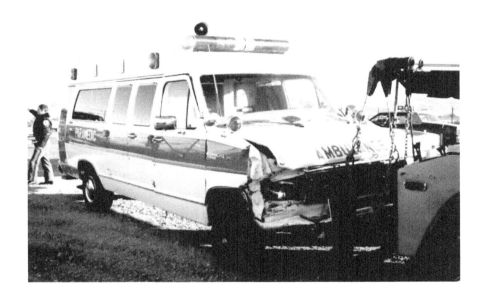

I was sick. This was my first accident driving an emergency vehicle. A 6-year good-driving EMS record broken.

Both Mercy and American Ambulance services have a policy that no matter whose fault it is, if you are in an accident, your driving privileges are suspended until you have an accident review board hearing by the company supervisors.

So for the next three weeks I did all the attending. This didn't bother me, but my pride was hurt and the other medics knew it and made sure I didn't forget it. While the crews gave me a hard time in good fun, the Senior Ambulance Mechanic (Frank) was spitting nails. When the wrecker delivered his ambulance to the mechanic shop, he let me have it with both barrels. He is from New York, with a strong Brooklyn accent. "What da fuck did you do to my ambulance!! I'm gonna kill you!" As he smacked the rather large wrench into the palm of his hand, the statement was rather believable!

Fortunately time heals all wounds and my pride was no exception. The world kept turning and I wasn't going to give up just because I had this setback.

The new year also marked a new year for teaching part-time at the Clark County Community College. This year, I was scheduled to teach the Emergency Medical Technician refresher course as well as several EMT through Paramedic classes. I was very excited about the teaching opportunities.

Despite my accident, American and Mercy Ambulance services respected my work and opinion, and requested that I sit on a panel of paramedics and dispatchers to review response times for all of Clark County. The goal, to reduce response times to under 8 minutes for 90% of all calls. Currently, the response time is under 8 minutes for 80% of all calls. That extra 10% is hard to come by. The meetings are very serious, in-depth, with every aspect of calls reviewed; time of day, areas of high volume, distances to the call, traffic congestion, and mechanical issues. Every facet that could impact an emergency response was assessed.

These meetings were real eye openers. I learned a lot about our service and where we were going as a company by sitting in these meetings. The pressure to come up with a plan was pretty intense. Not only did we need to come up with a plan that would improve response times, it had to be cost efficient, done with equipment already available and not only cause undue strain on the crews in the field, but try to relieve some stressors.

Superman thought he had a job keeping the world safe, he never worked for Mercy Ambulance!

I continued to lecture at High Schools on drunk driving, and they continue to go over extremely well. I'd been trying to get the lectures videotaped, but every time we scheduled with the cameraman, something came up and it got postponed.

January had been an extremely cold month for 'Sun belters". Temperatures had dipped into the 20s and even the teens on a few nights. We even had snow one very cold Sunday. I was so annoyed. I had moved to Las Vegas to get away from the snow and cold. I closed the curtains and grumbled to myself around the house. Robin had gone to Los Angeles for the weekend and I didn't want anything to do with the snow.

My American Ambulance paramedic partner, Paul Young, had introduced me to a young lady named Terry Kozlowski. Terry was bright and funny, and the step-daughter of the Regional Director for Pepsi-Cola-U.S.A. Terry called me at noon on this snowy day and said, "Have you looked outside lately?" I said, "No. And I ain't gonna!" She said, "It's snowing! And it's coming down in big flakes! Isn't it beautiful?" I said, "Sure! If you're an Eskimo! Snow is one of the reasons that I left Iowa! It's a curse! It followed me down here!" Terry said, "I know what your problem is. You've got the wrong attitude. If you don't like snow, act like it's not snowing." I said, "You know, you're right! I have a Jacuzzi in the backyard so let's have a Jacuzzi party!" We invited eight people over and sat outside in the Jacuzzi with the snow falling around us, drinking wine and getting tipsy. We then went inside and sat in front of the fireplace until the wee hours of the morning.

Terry was right, when something gets you down, don't ruminate on it, turn it into a positive!

The next evening, Robin came home and said, "I hear that it snowed." I said, "Yes. Thank God it melted." Robin asked, "Did you get a picture of it?" I said, "Hell no! I didn't even want to look at it, let alone take pictures of it." Robin just laughed.

A little bit more about Terry Kozlowski. She is a pre-med student at UNLV. We get along great, although she is as frightfully busy as I am. Neither of us want a permanent, full-time, relationship. Just someone to occupy our free time together when we want companionship. She comes from a fairly prominent Las Vegas family. Lots of power. She literally could get away with murder! I'm not kidding.

The call-volume during the month of January was ungodly high. Especially on my shifts. It started getting to the point that people dreaded coming to work when they knew they were working with me.

I was averaging 15 to 25 calls a shift. Not all of these were transports, of course, but they were still initial responses. I had a couple of shifts where I got to work and ran nonstop, back-to-back calls until I got off shift 24hrs later. Due to this high call volume and other teaching activities, I haven't been able to keep a day-to-day account of the activities at Mercy or American ambulance, so I'll try and hit the high points of the past few weeks.

Paul Young and I have been working together full-time for almost four months now and I couldn't be happier. We worked together on Tuesdays and Thursdays, then he worked with a part-time paramedic on Saturday and I worked with a part-time paramedic on Sunday. This had been our cycle for the past four months. We had become so comfortable with each other's actions that everything was second nature to us. At times, it was hard for the Fire Department paramedics to keep up with us. We always knew what the other was going to need even before being asked for it.

When Paul and I were between calls, and driving around our district, we loved to watch other people drive. Lord knows somebody needed to watch them drive, because most weren't paying attention or even realized they were behind the wheel of a vehicle. Now I'm not saying that Paul and I were superior human beings or anything, but at times we had to look for a long time before we found any signs of intelligent life in the cars around us.

An ambulance sits higher than a regular vehicle, so we can observe what is going on in vehicles around us without the occupants becoming aware. So what were people doing while they were supposed to be driving? They were reading books; fixing their hair or painting their fingernails; looking for items under the seat or in the backseat; one guy was even sitting in the passenger seat attempting to adjust the passenger mirror while driving down the road! We even caught several couples engaged in intimate acts that were better suited for the bedroom!

Things got more exciting when we turned on our red lights and siren. If we did this too suddenly, it took away the little sense of mentality and vehicle control these people had been able to muster and sent many into a panic. For example: One day we were traveling along a Vegas street at a normal rate of speed, moving with the flow of traffic, when we received an emergency call. The first thing we did was to turn on our red lights. Usually traffic would not notice, or maybe one person would notice and pull to the right and stop. The rest of the traffic would continue to drive around the stopped motorist and into our lane of travel without even looking in their rearview mirror. So now we turned on the siren, and everyone slammed on their brakes! Inevitably, a little old lady was in the car directly in front of us. She had her eyes glued to the rearview mirror and her foot firmly planted on her brake pedal, and just sat there looking at us. I usually pointed for her to pull her car to the right but she wouldn't understand. So I'd get on the public address system, "PULL YOUR CAR TO THE RIGHT... NO, YOUR OTHER RIGHT." Finally, she'd start to creep to the right at about half the speed she was traveling before we turn on our red lights and siren. It could drive you up the wall, if you didn't see the humor in it.

This happened on average five times a day. As we drove by these little old ladies who were staring bewildered up at us, I applauded them for their quick, decisive, maneuvering. Maybe next time they'd take a bus!

Paul and I were also avid girl watchers! While this is a year-round holiday destination, as the weather warmed up the outfits became more and more revealing. We always showed our appreciation by honking and waving. Paul is a sucker for a tall blonde, where I'm not as discriminating. I love anything with a beautiful figure. Paul and I know exactly where to sit in our district to catch a glimpse of the prettiest women in town.

Back to ambulance calls.

In the past few weeks, I've cared for a large number of critically ill patients. In the past month, Paul and I have responded to over a dozen cardiac arrests. We recently had three cardiac arrests in one day! People may not realize it, but resuscitating a cardiac arrest patient takes a lot out of a paramedic crew. Resuscitation efforts are extremely physical and intense. You really drain yourself due to the extreme mental and physical exertion. During a cardiac arrest call, the first team to arrive on the scene will determine if the patient's collapse is fresh enough to attempt resuscitation efforts or pronounce dead on the scene.

If the first team believes the patient is resuscitatable, they will begin CPR, provide cardiac shocks (Defibrillation) and try to intubate the patient. After CPR is started and the airway secured, the second crew will typically have arrived. Together, the two teams start an IV and give cardiac medications. While all this is going on, the person ventilating the patient, tries to get some background history from family members or bystanders that witnessed the event. If the patient doesn't begin to respond to initial drug therapy and defibrillations, the potential for them to survive drops considerably.

Regardless, we quickly secure them into the ambulance and scoot to the nearest hospital for the emergency room to continue resuscitation efforts or for the ER doctor to pronounce the patient "Dead On Arrival (D. O. A.)."

If the person starts to respond to drug therapy, resuscitation efforts intensify. We try additional meds to strengthen a weak pulse, or improve their blood pressure. It gets extremely intense at times keeping that delicate balance just right. If the blood pressure is too low blood perfusion to the brain is not enough; but if the pressure is too high, it wears out the heart.

By the time a cardiac arrest resuscitation case is brought into the hospital, a paramedic crew can use up most of the medications in their paramedic drug bag. Having to replace most of the drugs in your kit three times in one shift can be extremely time-consuming, not to mention the down time needed to clean up an ambulance after the patient has vomited, blood is spilled while starting additional IVs, and medication syringes are thrown all over the back of your Unit.

Not only have Paul and I responded to a large number of cardiac arrest, but we've also responded to dozens of unstable heart attack patients. Which in essence are the cardiac arrest patients just before their heart stops beating. These calls are just as intense as the cardiac arrests. The trick being to keep your patient alive and stable.

While Paul and I have lost a few patients, keeping them stable or bringing them back made us feel great. Having patients slip through our fingers, really hits us hard. We really cared about the patients in our charge and felt the losses deeply.

Medical emergencies weren't the only critical patients we saw in the past few weeks. We responded to an extremely bad motorcycle accident in which a guy riding a Harley Davison motorcycle hit a Cadillac head-on.

The Cadillac was moving at about 40 mph turning into a corner, when the driver of the motorcycle, intoxicated and high on drugs, smacked into the frontend of the Caddy at 70 mph. The impact threw him 250 feet behind the car and then he skidded another hundred feet down the road, then into the desert. The impact was so hard that it knocked the Cadillac backwards and sideways over 75 feet.

The driver of the Cadillac wouldn't have suffered any serious injuries had she been wearing her seatbelt, but she wasn't and the impact propelled her forward, driving her head through the front windshield.

The driver of the motorcycle was a mess. The initial impact split him open from his naval to his rectum. Both his legs were broken in multiple places; five or six ribs were fractured causing one lung to collapse; we also suspected he had a broken neck. The most shocking thing, however, was that the guy was still alive!

Upon arriving to the scene, we knew the guy would die before we could drive him to the hospital in our ambulance, so I called for the EMS helicopter, "Flight-For-Life". We then began an intense resuscitation effort. He had stopped breathing, so I intubated him.

We placed the pneumatic anti-shock trousers (M.A.S.T) on his lower extremities while the Fire Rescue crew started two large bore IVs.

The Sheriff's Search and Rescue crew were occupied with keeping the woman in the Cadillac stable while we worked on the motorcyclist. The EMS helicopter landed on the highway some 80 feet from the accident scene, and we turned over our care to the flight crew. The patient's blood pressure had starting to drop so they rushed him to the Valley hospital emergency room where he later went into full cardiac arrest and died due to massive internal injuries.

The driver of the Cadillac was extricated from her car and we took her by ground ambulance to the Valley hospital emergency room as well. She was later admitted to the hospital in stable condition.

Then there were the gunshot victims, most of them self-inflicted. One such case was for a 52-year-old female with an extensive history of cancer. Her pain was so unbearable that she attempted to shoot herself with a .38 caliber pistol in the head.

Head shots are so messy. They deform the face by making it swell up and bulge the eyes out; In addition, you have blood, brains and spinal fluid coming out the bullet holes, and this woman had all of the above. If it wasn't for the fact that she was still breathing, I would have pronounced her dead on the scene. Since she had a pulse and was breathing, we prolonged the inevitable by starting an IV and attempting to stabilize her. A new Fire Department paramedic was able to practice intubating her and then we made tracks for the closest hospital ER, where the doctor just let her go.

We also had our fair share of jerks. I hate that these idiots tend to stick out in my mind. They are the kind of people that think everyone else was put on this earth for the sole purpose of serving them, and they unfortunately tend to get under my skin.

On the flipside, there are many people that Paul and I think are absolute saints! It's amazing, because these are the ones that demand the least, but think we are the biggest heroes.

It's the people that are difficult and demanding, and for whom we work our butts off, that seem to think we were put here just to serve them.

7 AM Thursday, 7 March, 1985

Heavy sigh, once again I'm playing catch-up on my writing. Time seems to travel so quickly. My lectures have become very popular. High schools have written letters thanking me for my presentation and still more schools are asking me to come and talk. Things couldn't be going any better. I'm averaging two high schools a week, which is about as much as I can manage with my work schedule. Each lecture is to 1000 students per school. If things go according to plan, I should reach about seven or eight thousand students by the end of April.

Two weekends ago, I managed to take my International Scout out into the desert for a 4 x 4 adventure. I invited Terry Kozlowski to join me and we had a fun time. We drove to Needles, California and headed off the main highway along an old desert trail. After driving 50 or 60 miles along an isolated sandy wash, we stopped to make camp. The weather was beautiful, ranging from between 80 to 85°F during the day. We camped out under the stars and made a little bonfire. Just the two of us with the stars and the silent desert. It was a wonderfully relaxing evening.

The night sky in the desert was so beautiful. We camped without a tent and just looked up into the heavens. There was no light pollution, and the sky was crystal clear. You could see a million *more* stars in the desert sky than what one can see in or near any city. While it was great to be away from the city for the weekend and enjoy this extremely relaxing atmosphere, the weekend abruptly ended and I found myself back in the middle of all my work that Sunday afternoon.

The response time committee had found several interesting pieces of information about our system. One of those pieces concerned our dispatch system. While the members of our emergency dispatch team were dedicated individuals, none had been specifically trained to do what they did, and were working with outdated equipment. The solution was going to cost Mercy ambulance a substantial amount of money to update the equipment and provide adequate training for the dispatch team. The committee was confident in their findings, but concerned how Mercy's Executive leaders were going to take the news. Would they purchase the new $7000 computer and implement our new policies? Would people lose their jobs? Would the street medics feel that the report was an attack on them?

Paul and I were about to get off-shift this Friday (March 8th) morning when we received a call for a "nose problem" at the Office Bar, a drinking establishment a few blocks from the substation. After a while, you know exactly what type of person the patient is going to be. Just hearing the description of the call, location and the time of day tells you pretty much all you need to know.

This call came to us as an emergency response, but we didn't even bother. We strolled to the call, code 2 (non—emergency) to find this guy with a bloody nose standing by the Fire Department Rescue Unit. They saw us driving up and just waved us on by, it wasn't even worth stopping to ask what happened. We shook our heads, turned around and headed back for the substation.

After handing our ambulance over to our relief, I headed for a dental appointment. It was my first visit to a dentist in about ten years. I was not really excited about this decision, but I figured I'd better go and get it done. My dentist was also my Tae Kwon Do instructor, which was kind of nice since I get a discount when I see him in his dental office.

I drove home, changed clothes and chatted with my roommate Robin. She was in the process of packing for a long weekend in Los Angeles. Robin was a field paramedic that had suffered one too many back injuries and had been moved into administration. She had been assigned to the Phoenix, Arizona ambulance bidding process. The contract bidding process had been the focus of our conversation for the past few weeks. She related that they hadn't heard anything from Phoenix yet but that Mercy still had a 50-50 chance of getting the contract. If Mercy won the contract, Robin would be moving to Arizona to help set up operations there. If that happened, I would be losing a roommate once again.

I then headed for my dental appointment. "Jim-the-dentist" had a couple very cute assistants, and I enjoyed giving them a hard time while I waited for Jim to come check my teeth. All he did was look into my mouth and tell me what he wanted to do. What he wanted to do was going to cost me $400! Nine cavities! On a Paramedic budget, this was going to have to be done one tooth at a time.

Robin has been my roommate on Xavier street for about nine months. As I have related previously, I had initially moved into this house with paramedic Jim Cox six months after I arrived to Las Vegas. When Jim moved out, paramedic Bob Cochran replaced him. Bob was a nice enough guy, but smoked far too much pot. I don't think the guy could go several hours, let alone a whole day without lighting a joint. I'm no prude. I had tried marijuana. It simply wasn't my cup of tea. All it did was make me stuff my face with food and then go to sleep. Definitely not for me. He and Shelley Windholtz began to date. While I think Shelley initially would have preferred to date me, I was far too wrapped up in my work to give her the time and attention that she deserved. Bob, on the other hand, was more interested in her than work. When they first started dating, Bob asked me if his dating Shelley bothered me. I related that if Shelley was happy, I was happy. Their relationship quickly advanced into an engagement. That is when things started getting weird between Bob and I.

They were trying to scrape together money to pay for a wedding by using their half of the rent. That is when Bob fell out of favor. It was just at that time when I was having difficulty with Bob and Shelley, Robin was having roommate problems of her own. In fact, her incoming roommates were supposed to be my outgoing roommates! We compared notes and decided that we could resolve each other's roommate problems by booting Bob and Shelley and sharing a house ourselves.

That had been nine months ago, and for the most part, all my roommate issues had resolved. Robin had moved into my rented house on Xavier street and had brought with her a lot of very nice furniture. She paid her half of the rent and utilities on time, did not have crazy boyfriends, and was a very nice person to have around the house. While Robin was a great roommate, the house was not the best; it was poorly insulated, poorly maintained by the landlord, and the pool was beginning to have major issues. We needed to find a nicer place to live.

That afternoon, I went for a drive around several nicer neighborhoods to see what properties might be available for rent. While there were real estate agents that could have done this for me, I really didn't want to pay someone a commission that would cut into my ability to make the needed deposits on the new house. I drove around but didn't find anything that I liked.

That evening I joined Paul Young and a friend of his who was celebrating his birthday for a night of barhopping until the wee hours of the morning.

9:30 AM Saturday, 9 March, 1985

Terry called bright and early to wake me up. Despite the fact that I had only slept four hours, I felt refreshed. We went out shopping for new bucket seats to put into my scout. We ended up on the northside of town, out past the Nellis Air Force Base. While we were out browsing through junkyards, we were delighted to catch the Air Force Thunderbirds practicing their maneuvers. Bucket seats and a free air show what an awesome morning!

That afternoon, we picked up Terry's sister and her fiancé from the airport. Terry and her sister are a lot alike, even though they would never admit it. I was invited to their house that evening for homemade lasagna and a housewarming party at Terry's cousin's house. While the evening was fun, I found it difficult to converse with the folks gathered. Terry and her family belong to the upper crust of Las Vegas society. Their view of the world were somewhat twisted and not to my way of thinking. It was the first time I had been invited to their house, so I just smiled and said, "That is an interesting thought." And just moved on to speak to other people that ultimately shared similar points of view.

After the party, Terry and I drove to a high point overlooking the city lights. We sat and talked until just after midnight. Tomorrow was another work day.

8 AM Sunday, 10 March, 1985

I was working with paramedic Mike Gunter today. Mike is a part-time paramedic for both Mercy and American ambulance services. He worked full time out at the Nevada Nuclear Test site. Mike had a very good street reputation, and I was eager to work with him and to pick his brain about what he did at the Nuclear Test Site.

The day started off hectic with four transports in the morning, but dropped to a standstill in the afternoon. Mike had a ton of college studying to do, so he enjoyed the quiet afternoon. I, on the other hand, was bored. I had only brought a minimal amount of work with me in my briefcase, which I had completed in an hour and a half.

Later in the afternoon, Mike's wife, Amy, came to the substation to visit us. I had met Amy at Mercy's main headquarters previously, and had found her to be a very pleasant person. Mike was also a very pleasant guy to be around, but put these two together and you got instant conflict. Amy had been there five minutes and they were at each other's throats. Mike and Amy had been married two years, of which seven months, they had been separated from each other.

Unfortunately, most of the married couples I knew were experiencing the same problems. They all told me it was because of the work we did. But that story didn't compute with me. They didn't really see enough of each other to get tired of each other's company. I mean, it looked more like dating to me. You get to see each other every other day or in some cases even less.

I wasn't even sure where they found the time to be together long enough to create stuff to argue about! After Amy left, Mike told me that it was Amy's fault. That she just didn't understand the work that he did. Amy said she did, but Mike just couldn't seem to handle the pressures of married life. What a life. To go home just to listen to your spouse argue with you. I could never handle a relationship like that, nor would I put up with it. I must have been doomed to be single for life. At least for the next few years, anyway.

Sadly, Robin was also having problems with her boyfriend. Maybe it was something in the water!

The rest of the nightshift was uneventful. We had a guy that tripped and fell down a flight of steps at the Dunes casino and broke his ankle. As usual, he was just getting into town and hadn't even checked into his room.

Our last call came in at around 2:30 AM. The call was for possible overdose. We were given the correct address, (which was in a very large low-income apartment complex), but the apartment number given was vague. We walked around this crime-ridden apartment complex trying to find the right apartment. Two white guys in an exclusively black neighborhood. As I was walking through the dirt central court yard of the apartment complex, I heard a couple screaming at each other and I figured the commotion was probably the address we were looking for.

The brawling couple were in an upstairs apartment. As I walked up the stairs toward the door, I heard breaking glass, more yelling and the two running around inside the home. I yelled over to the Metro police officers that had just arrived on-scene that I had found the apartment. As Metro approached the apartment door, we knocked. There was a pause in the commotion but then it started up again, but was moving closer to the door.

When the couple reached the door, it opened long enough for us to see an elderly black man with a younger woman on his back. The door then slammed shut in our face. Metro police pounded on the door again, but no one came back to the door. The police officer put his boot into the door, splintering the door frame, and swinging the door wide open.

There in full view, was a guy in his late 50s trying to wrestle a girl in her early 20s off his back. The girl was only wearing a bra and panties and the guy was only wearing underwear, which were around his ankles. I looked at the two wrestling around the apartment, and then looked over at the police officer who was shaking his head in disgust. A moment later, we had the two split.

We gave the girl a blanket and told the guy to pull up his shorts. Metro police were familiar with the girl; they had been called to a different address, where her boyfriend lived, for disturbance calls. This particular incident started when she had an argument with her boyfriend and had decided to move in with this guy, who supposedly was going to employ her as an accountant. I don't know what started the argument, but she started breaking up the apartment and we were called.

Totally flustered, we left the situation in the hands of Metro police, who had decided that somebody was going to jail, they weren't sure who yet, but somebody.

Mike and I cleared the call and went back to the substation.

7:30 AM rolled around and our relief arrived. I was on my way home at 08:10 AM.

Once home, I made a light breakfast and thought about the last call of the day. Specifically, I thought about that snapshot in time when the door flew open and we saw this couple in the most unflattering pose possible. I really knew nothing about those two people or what lead up to that moment, but that image will be forever imprinted in my mind.

I wondered how many times people had witnessed me and my actions for only a fleeting second; a lasting imprint of my actions, good or bad, forever rendering an opinion of who they thought I was.

I vowed to remember that moment and to remember that as I respond to emergencies across this city, there are a thousand people a day taking snapshots of my behavior as well.

8 - THE BIG ONE

6 PM Thursday, 4 April, 1985

Finally, work and life have slowed down long enough for me to write. Since I last wrote, I'd been named to a new committee in addition to the Response Time Committee, the Communications Committee. Both tried to demand my undivided attention, but were satisfied with whatever spare time I could offer. My lectures continued to be favorably received by high schools across the city, and now I was starting to talk to groups outside of high school students.

On May 14th, I would be the main speaker at an alcohol and driving related insurance program being held at the Palace Station Casino, which meant I would have to change my lecture to appeal to a more general audience. Unfortunately, I was still struggling to get the lecture videotaped. I think it came down to the fact that I was asking the cameraman to volunteer his time, like I volunteered my time to present. Unfortunately, I got bumped every time he had a paying gig!

Robin and I finally found the house we were looking for! One with an extra bedroom for guests as well as one we could turn into an office. The catch was that we were seven days away from the end of my current lease on Xavier. That gave us two days to pack and move out, two days to clean the old house, and then another three days to ready the new place, and move in! All while still working our regular shifts. The work demands had us moving and cleaning the houses at rather strange hours of the night. But this was Las Vegas. I don't think anyone even noticed!

The move-in week was a whirlwind and I was exhausted. While we were technically in the new house, the only items really set up were the beds. It would take a month to get stuff put away and the house decorated.

The month of March also had its share of memorable calls. One of the biggest calls of my paramedic career happened the night I was supposed to go to Reno Nevada to help a fellow paramedic move in with his girlfriend. The move was postponed and I ended up covering an American Ambulance shift.

It was the evening of Friday, March 29, 1985.

I started this shift at 8 AM with American ambulance paramedic David Duritsa. We ran back-to-back calls all day long. We were really running our butts off. We'd clear from one call and be immediately given our next. We'd clear from a code 2 (non-emergency) transfer and then head for an automobile accident. We'd just get done with that and head for an assault. Upon clearing the assault, we'd head for a heart attack victim. The majority of the calls were significant medical or traumatic emergencies, yet all those calls seemed insignificant after we had cleared from "The Big One".

You hear paramedics across the U.S. using that phrase: "The Big One." It typically refers to a significant mass casualty incident. Paramedics leaving a party can often be heard calling back to their friends, "Good night guys, I'll see you at the Big One." But only a few ever get called to "The Big One." Well, that night Dave and I did.

It had just struck midnight when Dave and I finally made it back to our substation. The grueling day of back-to-back calls seemed to have abated. Neither of us could recall having a day quite as intense as this day had been. We collapsed onto our substation beds and kicked off our shoes. It felt so nice to be able to stretch out and relax. My back ached from all the heavy lifting from the vehicle extrications, CPR and patient transports we had performed that day.

I closed my eyes and was instantly asleep. Dave had also quickly fallen asleep. We had only been asleep a few minutes when the pager sounded for another emergency call. The time was 00:30hrs and we groaned as we heard the dispatcher advise that we would be responding to Whiskey Pete's casino at the Nevada/California State line for two patients complaining of back pain from an earlier automobile accident. Visions of some old couple complaining of neck pain and lawsuits kept running through my mind.

Dave and I dragged ourselves out of the substation and into the ambulance and begrudgingly went en route. Again, we heard the dreaded call repeated, "One Medic 3, respond code 3 to Whiskey Pete's Casino for a 421: back problem resulting from an earlier 401." I said, "Medic 3, 10-4 responding Code 3."

Ah yes, Whiskey Pete's, the last casino in Nevada. It sits right at the state line between California and Nevada. Some 25 miles from Las Vegas. Considering travel time to the casino, patient assessment, and travel time to the hospital, there would be no way we would make it back to our substation before 2 AM.

We departed the substation and headed south on Interstate 15.

Dispatch was once again on the radio with us. "One medic 3, control" I said, "Medic 3". Dispatch relayed, "New information has been reported to us that this is a Greyhound bus versus a Semi-truck 401. Please advise on your arrival, the number of injuries. Flight-for-life EMS helicopter is also responding. Las Vegas Fire Department is also responding Units 9, 87, 11, 90, ex-83, and 86, do you copy?" I replied, "10-4. How many injuries do they think they have?" Dispatch replied, "They believe they have two dead, seven critical and 25 others with injuries." I looked over at Dave as he was looking over at me. I said, "Shit! 32 injured! Dave, just out of curiosity, what form of triage did you learn in your paramedic program?" We talked triage and mass casualty management as we raced to the scene. I would handle the initial triage of patients and Dave would handle communications, ambulance placement and transports. We both knew that we would be the first Unit on-scene and the success of the entire mass casualty incident would depend upon us.

We arrived on-scene twenty minutes after the call was dispatched. As we pulled into the casino parking area, we were directed to three separate motel rooms accessible only from the outside. The accident had happened three miles south of Whiskey Pete's on the California side of the state-line, along a steep grade of road leading down to the Casino. We learned that a loaded 18-wheeler had lost control and smashed to the back of a bus full of senior citizens heading to Las Vegas for a weekend junket. The bus lost control, left the road and fell into a square drainage ditch. The bus was probably going 80 miles an hour when it hit the ditch and came to an immediate stop. Several passengers were ejected through the front windshield and then the bus rolled over on them. An empty bus had picked up the walking wounded as well as everyone they could carry, and brought them to Whiskey Pete's.

Dave was already on the radio advising dispatch to send the next in-service Unit to the actual accident site to check for survivors. The EMS helicopter was also flying to the accident site. I directed my attention to the injured people in the three motel rooms.

As I stepped into the first room twenty people all started screaming for my attention. "Help! Help! My wife is hurt badly. Please take care of her first!" Loved ones were grabbing at my arm trying to pull me in one direction or another. It was uncontrolled chaos.

There were injured and bleeding accident victims everywhere and everyone needed attention. In a loud, but calm voice, I asked everyone to calm down and be quiet for a second. Amazingly, they all complied. I then stated that a dozen more ambulances were en route and my job was to make the initial assessment so that the sickest could go first, but that everyone would get cared for quickly. With the group calmed down, I started working my way around the first room from right to left, performing my initial triage and treatment, only stopping to take care of severe bleeding, opening airways, and treating for shock. As I finished the first room, I went to the second and then third rooms.

I had just finished my initial evaluation when the next ambulance crew arrived. Two paramedics rushed to my side and asked, "What do you have, and how many?" I said, "I have seven critical that need to go by ambulance immediately, and another 30 that need to be stabilized and evaluated at an emergency room. Take this man and that woman first. He has a head injury and is unconscious with an unsecured airway. Her blood pressure is dropping and she has a rigid abdomen."

As subsequent paramedic teams arrived, I gave similar instructions. As I pointed each patient out I noted, "Each one has a completed triage tag with the extent of injuries listed on them. I've only completed a primary survey, so complete a full secondary survey and recheck vitals. Some conditions may have changed." I then started on my second round of evaluations, spinning off patients to awaiting ambulance crews until we were down to just the most minor of injuries.

The entire mass casualty response ran smoothly. By the time I had all the non-ambulatory (people that couldn't walk) patients loaded into ambulances, Dave had all the ambulatory patients loaded into a bus with instructions on where the bus driver was to take them.

I jumped into the back of my ambulance to find it had been stripped of every piece of equipment caring for this mass casualty event. Dave and I loaded the last two non-ambulatory patients into our ambulance and headed for Desert Springs Hospital ER. I had started this accident with almost 50 patients to worry about. I now had only two patients left.

Dave jumped into the driver seat, with the last remaining ambulatory victim in the passenger seat. With a sigh of relief he asked, "Are you ready?" I said, "Let's go," and with that we were en route to Desert Springs hospital.

En route to the hospital, I reviewed what I had written earlier on the two triage cards for the women in the back of my ambulance. One had a possible tibia and hip fracture, while the other had a possible spinal cord injury and was complaining of a loss of feeling in her left leg, as well as abdominal pain. I now reassessed her abdomen. It was rigid. *Shit!* I thought to myself. Her initial blood pressure on the triage card was 100 by palpation, but had now dropped to 80 by palpation. I peeked up front and whispered to Dave to get us into town as fast as possible. I placed her on oxygen via a non-rebreather mask, applied medical anti-shock trousers (MAST) and attempted to start an IV line. Her veins had collapsed and at 100 miles an hour, it was just too difficult.

Being alone in the back of an ambulance with two patients, one critical, is a handful. Fortunately, both patients remained stable for the trip into Desert Springs hospital.

Once in the hospital, we dropped off our patients and started restocking. By the time we had restocked all our equipment and had gotten gas, it was 4:30 AM. The adrenaline surge that had propelled us forward at the beginning of this call was now completely gone.

Dave and I were running on fumes both physically and emotionally. A mass casualty incident requires 200% of your physical and emotional energy. You have to be hypervigilant to every little thing that is going on around you so that you don't miss the subtle findings. It is not the person yelling at you that you must worry about, but the one sitting quietly in a corner. People care about their loved ones and they will do whatever it takes to get your attention to take care of them first, no matter how minor their injury may be. You must be able to wade through this physical and emotional chaos with the ability to pinpoint where the greatest need is.

We tried to review the call as we drove back to the substation, but we were just too tired. Fortunately, dispatch placed us in reserve and allowed us to get some desperately needed sleep. I needed those two hours of sleep. I was to lecture at the Clark County Community College all day once we finished our shift.

In addition to this mass casualty call, there were several other emergency responses of note:

Mike Gunter and I responded to an apartment complex called "The Vegas Towers", a large multistory complex home to extremely wealthy Jewish families.

We had received the call as a woman unable to move. We arrived on scene to find an elderly woman lying in bed with an apparent right-sided stroke. Her husband explained that two months ago, she fell and broke her hip and hadn't been able to walk without help since then. She now lay in bed, unable to move her entire right side.

Apparently after her hip surgery a blood clot formed in her leg and slowly migrated to her brain. The story was a sad one and unfortunately even more distressing than I initially thought.

In the 1920s, my patient was known as "Miss Stanley", the lead dancer of the Ziegfeld Follies and from the photos and newspaper clippings that they showed me, she was quite a beauty. Now, she was unable to do even the simplest of tasks without help. We took her to Desert Springs hospital. Both she and her husband were two of the nicest people you could meet. Miss Stanley was simply lovely. She would have had every right to be distressed and upset, but she was the exact opposite. I had a pleasant conversation with her all the way to the hospital. As I dropped her off at the hospital, I gave her a hug and related that while I wished I had met her when she was younger, I was honored to have met her today.

I recently spoke at four high schools and was surprised to find two teens in the audience that I had recently transported. One would initially think that that is a bad thing, but it turned out that they were interested in sharing their stories with the audience, which amplified the impact of the lecture.

I also responded to several teens after the lectures. The first was a 16-year-old male that was a passenger in a two-car vehicle accident. No alcohol or drugs were involved, just a careless driver. As I approached the wrecked car containing the teen, he recognized me right away and said "I haven't been drinking!! I wasn't driving, it wasn't my fault! I promise, I'll be more careful from now on! I know I should have listened!"

I gave him a reassuring smile and began assessing him for injuries. He had been extremely lucky. The impact site was on the passenger side but he had worn his seatbelt and came out relatively unscathed. His chief complaint was back and shoulder pains. His examination revealed a possible collarbone fracture. I immobilized his neck and placed a sling and swath around his shoulder to stabilize the collarbone. We extricated him from the vehicle and headed for the hospital.

During the ride to the hospital, I decided to have a little talk with him to reaffirm some of the points in my lecture. I said, "You know you were really, really lucky, wearing your seatbelt and all. Without it, you could have been thrown from the vehicle and killed. Do you remember what I said about not riding with people who are acting like jerks behind the wheel?" He said, "Yes, but he's a buddy of mine. I needed him to get home." I said, "Buddy or not, at least you wouldn't be going home by way of an ambulance ride and hospital visit, right?" He nodded his head in agreement. I said, "Listen. I'm not here to say I told you so. Somethings just happen and you are going to have to live with the consequences of it. But in the future, you can control your destiny. You have the right to choose to get into a car or not; to hang out with people that are bad for you or not. It is all your choice. In this instance, when your buddy was driving like a jerk, you could've told him to stop. He'd have either straightened up or he'd have told you, 'if you don't like the way I'm driving, get out!' If he'd have told you to get out, I would have considered him a real friend and taken his advice."

He stayed pretty quiet for the rest of the trip to the hospital, but just as we were pulling into the hospital he said (more to himself, I think) "Man that was a real stupid move." I just smiled and said, "Remember, self-preservation, take care of Number One first."

The second teen that had sat through my lecture wasn't even involved in an auto accident. He was a 16-year-old boy having girl problems and decided that he wasn't getting enough attention, so he shot himself in the abdomen with a .25 caliber pistol. Real smart kid, right? Luckily, he shot himself in the left lower abdominal quadrant at an angle that missed practically everything.

As I walked into the room where he lay, he looked up and said, "I remember you. You talked at my school. I said, "Oh? Do you remember all the things that I talked about regarding treatment in my ambulance and at the hospital? Well your case will be almost the same, except that shooting victims can sometimes be worse." He started to look very worried and asked, "You mean I don't get no painkillers?" I shook my head, "No painkillers." He asked "Are they gonna stick those big needles into my arms?" I said, "No. _I'M_ gonna stick those needles into your arms. The hospital's going to stick one of those big needles into your belly. Do you remember what I told you about internal abdominal bleeding?" He started to look even more worried and a little pale and nodded his head in affirmation.

I started two large bore IVs and placed him in medical anti-shock trousers (MAST) as a precautionary measure, and then headed towards the hospital. Just before we loaded him into the ambulance, the girl in question came up to our patient all misty eyed and bid him her undying love and that he was not to die so that they could live happily ever after.

I shook my head and rolled my eyes. While en route to the hospital, my patient began feeling the true impact of his injuries. The attention he initially craved was no longer fun and the pain he was now feeling was overriding everything. As he squirmed uneasily on the ambulance cot, he looked over at me and said, "Pretty stupid thing to do?" I said, "Yep, a pretty stupid thing to do. You've made your parents insane with worry, not to mention the large hospital bills they are going to receive from your stupid little stunt. And for what? Because this girl friend of yours was giving you the cold shoulder? What are you going to do the next time she gets a little upset? Wreck the family car? Pour gas all over yourself and light on fire? That would really get her attention! Son, there's one thing you've got to realize right now about girls. The swath is too wide and too deep to worry about any single one, especially at your age."

This teen's mom was riding in the front passenger seat of the ambulance crying and constantly looking back asking, "Is he okay? He's not dying, is he?" I'd say, "No ma'am he's fine." My patient was really starting to hurt and asked, "What's going to happen to me when I get to the hospital?" I said, "Well, when we get to the hospital, we are going to take you into the emergency room. Once there, a surgeon will come down and examine you." He looked at me wide-eyed and asked, "A surgeon!? You mean I've got to have surgery?!" I looked at him incredulously and said, "Son, you have a bullet hole in your gut. What did you think was going to happen once we got to the hospital?" I added, "By the way, when was the last time you ate?" He answered, "About an hour ago." I said, "That's too bad. They will have to stick a suction tube down your nose and into your stomach to clean all that food out before surgery. If you throw up, it might go into your lungs. They will also have to put a tube from your penis into your bladder to check for blood in your urine before surgery as well."

My patient was really starting to feel sorry for himself and asked, "Please have them knock me out before they do all that stuff. I don't know if I can handle any more pain!" I said, "Listen, like I told you in my lecture, they don't do all this stuff to be mean, they do it to keep you alive! There is one thing you have got to remember, whether you thought of this before you shot yourself or not. You could have and can still die! Everything that we do centers around that single thought. Keeping you alive, regardless of how much pain it causes you and believe me it could get a lot worse. He looked at me through misty eyes and said, "Am I going to die?" I said, "Not in my ambulance."

We then arrived to the emergency room where everything that I had forewarned him about came true, plus a couple of things that I knew they would probably do, but didn't want to scare him any further.

Upon entering the emergency department, a surgeon was standing-by. Dr. Terry Lewis, who was a very good friend. The teen's vital signs had remained stable during the transport and the MAST trousers, which had not been inflated, were taken off. A Foley catheter (tube that goes into your bladder) was inserted; a nasogastric tube (that runs down your nose into your stomach) was also inserted; x-rays were taken and then Dr. Lewis started his abdominal exam, which included a belly tap (needle inserted into the abdomen to look for blood); Dr. Lewis also used a sterile finger to insert into the bullet hole to track the path that the bullet took into the abdomen. And as I explained to my patient on the ride in, this was all done without painkillers.

> *I've got to add this little note right here and now, otherwise I'll forget about it. I'm writing while at work at substation on the American ambulance service. A little earlier this evening, my partner (Paul Young) was out in the front yard of our substation talking to the neighbors. He had left the door open and a sparrow flew into the substation and landed on the couch, and just sat there. He didn't fly away when we walked in or seem bothered by anything. Paul placed a few breadcrumbs by the bird and then started in on his college homework. Several hours later, the bird was still sitting there, just watching him. I for one, am not overly impressed with sparrows, and was ready to throw Paul's little feathered friend out! But Paul insisted that he would be all right. Paul then took his shirt off and laid it down by the sparrow. The bird hopped up on to Paul's shirt and went to sleep, but not before taking a healthy dump all over it! Talk about a metaphor in life! Paul had fallen asleep before the bird bestowed his gratitude on Paul's shirt, so he doesn't know it yet. I've been trying to keep the roar of laughter down so as not to wake up Paul or the bird! I can't wait for his reaction when he does!*

Life around Mercy and American ambulance services had remained unchanged. The turnover in paramedics and emergency medical technicians remained high. I guess that was to be expected from a service with such a high call volume. Many people hit their one year anniversary and applied elsewhere; some to the Nevada Test Site, others to the Clark County Fire Department, or any other place that paid more for less hours and fewer calls. There were so many new people, that when I saw an ambulance with people I didn't know in it, I just assumed they were new hires. A person could steal an ambulance, put on a blue shirt and I'd never know the difference! That's how bad it was becoming.

Mercy had really assumed the attitude of "something for nothing", they thought that they could get medics to do different events for nothing, when in turn the company was getting paid big bucks. It was not going over very well. Sentiment had zero cash value and if the company was making money from my medical skills, I wanted a piece of the pie.

Robin Nunn and I finally unpacked and settled into our new house at 4012 Stormcrest Street. We were very pleased with the way everything looked. We had twice the room and it was just a nice place to come home to after a tough shift at work.

My personal life had been having its ups and downs. I was casually seeing a few different girls on a routine basis. All of them wanted all of my time, and having as few days off as I did presented a very large problem. Especially on those days when I wanted to be left alone. One of them was always calling and wanting to come over or do something.

To review the list, I was still seeing Terry Kozlowski. She was typically in school on a lot of the days that I was off, which helped some. Liz was a secretary at one of the hospital emergency rooms and remained content with seeing me there and on the occasional date when time allowed. Tammy was also a secretary at another hospital and was also content with seeing me in her emergency room and out as time allowed. Kathleen was an emergency medical technician that just started working for Mercy ambulance. She was the first girl that I'd ever dated that was actually taller than I am! I'm a little over six feet tall, but she was a showgirl at a couple of the casinos downtown and was in excellent shape. Talk about legs!! She could have been with the Radio City Rockettes!

So far everything had been working out fine. They all knew that I saw other women, which some were not happy about, but they accepted it. Each was trying to figure out how to carve as much time as possible out of my schedule, as well as undermine the character of the other girls they knew I was seeing. It made life interesting and kept me on my toes. Besides, this was Las Vegas, "Where dreams came true!"

A great place to let your "Dreams come true", was at the Sunrise Hospital Fantasy Party.

This was a party hosted by the Sunrise hospital emergency department. People came dressed as their favorite fantasy. In the emergency medicine and prehospital healthcare arena, this was considered the party of the year. People went absolutely crazy! No holds barred! People made some of the craziest costumes. I had seen people dressed as Hugh Hefner, or an upstairs chambermaid. One woman came wrapped in nothing but saran wrap (she said she was just "leftovers") I had seen a fairy godmother - able to make your every wish come true; Tarzan and Jane; an assortment of punk rockers, gigolos, and hookers, and other outrageous costumes. They had live bands playing, magicians, Belly Dancers and even paid strippers! (There were even a few "non-paid" strippers!)

I arrived to the party at around midnight. I had been teaching at the community college all day and had just gone to the party in regular clothes. Amid this extremely bizarre crowd, I looked out of place! It didn't take long for partygoers to start altering my attire. Party beads from one person, a funny hat from another, a magic wand of my own from the fairy godmother. In an instant, I had been transformed to fit into this fantasy world.

The emergency room doctors at Sunrise hospital had established this party as a means for emergency medical personnel to blow off steam, reduce stress, and have fun with colleagues and peers, who often dealt with some of the hardest situations in life. I don't know when the first party was held, but it had been so successful that a tradition was instantly born.

This evening's party was just as epic as I imagined the very first party had been. Everyone was drinking and dancing, teasing and joking, flirting and chasing each other around the large yard. There were no fees for this party, nor requirement to bring anything to eat or drink. The only requirement was that you were a member of the Las Vegas EMS team. The emergency room docs at Sunrise hospital had paid for everything.

I found a beer, and then meandered around the party to see who I knew. There were a lot of hospital ER staff, a handful of ambulance people, as well as Fire Department and Las Vegas Police officers (all off-duty, and dressed in unimaginable costumes). As I walked through the crowd, someone grabbed my arm, spun me around, and gave me a big kiss! Talk about being delightfully surprised! It was René, a laboratory technician from Sunrise Hospital. She was dressed in a punk rocker outfit, and was extremely bored because there was no one she knew at the party when she arrived. She was thrilled to see me come through the door and eager to show me her gratitude!

We drank, danced, and talked through most of the evening (or should I say morning). But then the friends that she had come to the party with wanted to go home. Unfortunately, she had to bid me farewell and left the party. It was going to be daylight soon, and I figured I should probably head home as well. Just as I was heading for the exit, Liz, the former showgirl, snuck up behind me and grabbed my butt! She had just gotten off shift, and the party was starting to die down, so Liz and I left to find breakfast.

A great place for breakfast in the wee hours of the morning was at a location called, "Batista's Hole-in-the-wall" This was "Mob Central"! The place was always full of real-life "Good Fellas" that <u>loved</u> their Fire Department and Ambulance folks. I had met several people there that I would have never wanted to meet in a dark alley. That being said, I had always been treated with nothing but respect and courtesy here. Breakfast at Batista's cost next to nothing and depending on the crowd, was often free! It was almost 6 AM before I got home. I swear, it must have taken me a week to recover from that party!

I'm glad that I did recover from the party, because the next week my mother (Penny Klingensmith) and grandmother (Wynola 'Hoby" Vining) flew into town to visit. They were flying in on a Wednesday evening and leaving late Saturday night. I was off work on that Wednesday, Thursday, and Saturday, but had to work a 24hr shift on the Friday, while they were still in town. I didn't know if they expected to see all of Las Vegas in virtually two days, but that is exactly what we did!

On Wednesday evening, they arrived into Las Vegas at 10:45 PM. Robin and I drove them down to the Las Vegas strip to see all the lights. A few things had changed since mom visited me right after I had arrived. I pointed out a few of the changes as we drove downtown. After the initial tour, we drove to the house and dropped off their luggage. Grandma Vining was pretty tired, so she went to bed. Mom changed into fresh clothes and we went out to give the town a closer look.

I drove her to an area that overlooked the city for a view of the Vegas lights. We then drove down to Fremont street and toured the newly remodeled Golden Nugget casino. I jokingly asked mom if she was ready to stay up till 5 in the morning. She confirmed that she would be in bed long before that time! I just laughed. We toured the downtown casinos for a while, played a few slot machines, and then continued our tour along the Vegas strip.

I pointed out such landmarks as St. Vincent's Dining Hall (our local transit refugee home), a cardboard shanty town, the Cuban Mafia community, as well as a few other "attractions" that never quite make it into the Las Vegas guidebooks. I then took her to the top of the Landmark Hotel where she took additional pictures of the city lights. The Landmark bar was closed, so I took her to another little bar not too far away called the Peppermill. By the time, we returned home I had to laugh. I said, "Mom! Do you know what time it is?" She said, "Not really." I said, "Well, it's 3 o'clock in the morning here or 5 o'clock in the morning back in Iowa! I told you I was going to keep you up until 5 in the morning!"

I woke up at 10 AM to find mom and grandma already awake. After a quick shower, we headed down to the Holiday Casino buffet to have breakfast. After breakfast, we drove to Lake Mead. While there were a few high clouds and a bit of haze in the air, the lake looked beautiful. Deep blue against a red, rugged Rocky backdrop. We toured the South Shore Road of the lake, then drove to the Hoover Dam. Once at the Dam, we walked along the top and reflected upon this construction marvel. We then drove through Henderson and over to the Red Rocks south of town. The drive was extremely picturesque, with wild burros often loitering along the roadside begging for a few morsels from the tourists. It was almost 5 PM as we headed back to the house. We ate a quick meal, showered, and then headed off to the Imperial Palace Casino to see the show "Legends in concert". Terry Kozlowski also joined us for the performance. It was almost 1:30 AM when I got everyone home and to bed!

6 AM Friday, 12 April, 1985

I worked a 24-hour shift with Dave Duritsa. It seemed like every time I worked with Dave, we had a killer shift, and this Friday was no different. I had started the shift pretty tired from touring family members, but after running one call after another all shift long, I was beyond exhausted. I had to sleep until about noon to recover before continuing the "Southern Nevada Tour".

Noon, Saturday, 13 April, 1985

I started the Saturday tour by going to the buffet at the Circus Circus Casino and Hotel. After eating breakfast, grandma said she didn't feel up to traveling to Mount Charleston, so we headed back toward the house. Along the way, I pointed out Siegfried and Roy's mansion as well as the ghettos that kept us busy at Mercy. After getting grandma settled into the house, mom and I headed for Mount Charleston and the Lee Canyon ski area.

It was quite unique during this time of the year in Southern Nevada. It could be 90°F in the Valley, yet people could still snow skiing up on the mountain. We drove up into the snowy ski resort, and toured the beautiful Canyon Lodge. After having a cup of coffee, we headed back down the mountain through Kyle Canyon and down into the warm 90°F Valley. During the drive, I told mom about all the accidents and death that had happened there. I think it was a part of the tour she could have done without.

Upon returning to town, we then drove to Sam's Town Hotel and Casino where she did some shopping. With her shopping needs met, we turned around and headed back to the house to get ready for another Las Vegas show and their return flight back to the "Great White North".

Before heading for the show, we ate at the house and they packed their luggage. The evening's show was at the Silver Slipper Casino along the middle of the Vegas Strip. It was a Vegas burlesque show called "Boy-lesque", a female impersonation show and extremely funny. The female look-alikes were remarkable.

One guy was the spitting image of Cher, and another looked like Liza Minnelli.

We enjoyed the evening but still had a couple of hours to kill before we had to head for the airport, so I drove them to the MGM Grand Hotel, had a couple of drinks and then toured the Hotel's luxury shops on the ground floor.

Finally, it was time to head for the airport, where they caught a flight back to Kansas City. I don't know about mom and grandma, but I was definitely worn out from their three day adventure.

9 - THE MAIN EVENT

6 AM Monday, 15 April, 1985

I began a 12-hour shift with Mike Manning (a Las Vegas city Fire Department paramedic). Thank God it was a slow shift and I was able to recuperate from the past whirlwind weekend!

3 PM Monday, 15 April, 1985

This evening was the "Marvelous" Marvin Hagler - Tommy "Hitman" Hearns - Caesar's Palace, pay-per-view, undisputed middleweight championship of the world boxing match!

Paul Young and I were on stand-by for this world-famous boxing match. Several other Mercy ambulance paramedic teams were also in attendance. Paramedic teams David Skoff and Don Abshire, Bob Cochran and Dennis Lee were positioned around the boxing event.

Paul and I were assigned to work ring-side for this event, which was where all the newscasters, reporters, celebrities, and boxing teams sat. Paul was a close friend of the boxing federation's ringside physician (Dr. Don Romeo) and attended as many boxing matches as he could. He had autographs from many famous boxers such as Larry Holmes, Hector "Macho" Camacho, Ray 'Boom Boom' Mancini, as well as the two main fighters that were going head-to-head this evening. Being ringside at such a major evens also allowed Paul to get autographs from movie stars such as Bo Derek, Don Rickles and Joan Rivers.

The ring-side section was known as the "Blue Section". All these seats were complementary seats, which meant no one had to pay, but they were not given to just anyone. These were the VIP of the VIP seats!

The section behind the blue section was called the "Pink section". These tickets ran from $650 to $1000 per seat. This was the section that I was assigned to monitor. I was sitting in a $1000 seat! (Which was a hell of a lot more money than what I was making that night or even that week!) Sitting next to me was Cheech Marin of "Cheech and Chong fame" and on the other side of me was Tommy Hearns' younger brother, who looked almost identical to his older brother, only slightly shorter.

I felt like a pauper in this crowd. There was more gold and money floating around than I had ever seen in my entire life. I witnessed one guy bet another guy $10,000 on Hearns, and then handed it to him in cash to hold the bet! I about lost it right there.

Everyone had at least two or three gold and diamond rings. I was also getting a kick out of watching what looked like an overdressed football crowd sitting on regular bleachers with binoculars. Patrons in expensive dresses and suits, eating hors d'oeuvres and drinking champagne.

There were several boxing matches that preceded the main event. The first bout of the evening was a middleweight fight involving two unknowns. It was an even match, which ended in a knockout in the fourth round. The defeated fighter had been so soundly rendered unconscious that we ended up having to respond into the ring to render first aid.

He had his bell soundly rung and had lost control of his airway. We stabilized him onto a long backboard and inserted a nasal pharyngeal airway to keep him breathing smoothly. He needed to be transported to the hospital for a head CT scan, but since Paul and I were on ringside duty we transferred him to Don and Dave for transport to the hospital after stabilization.

They were not pleased. They wanted to take our spot in order to see the main event up close, but the ringside physician (Dr. Romeo) closed the argument by saying that Paul and Ty would be the ones staying. So begrudgingly Don and Dave headed for their ambulance with the semi-comatose boxer.

The next three fights were great entertainment, but uneventful from a medical standpoint. The entire seating arena was packed by the time the main event got underway.

I cannot even imagine how much money Caesar's Palace made on an event like this. Prices for seats went from $1000 for near ringside seats, $650-$250 for the bleacher seats, and $50 just to watch it on cable TV inside the casino! It was labeled as "The Fight of the

Century," a Don King sponsored prizefight that he had titled "The War."

This definitely was "<u>The</u> fight"! When the match started, Hector "Macho" Camacho was standing beside me and we were sharing a pair of binoculars that Paul had brought along. Hector got to jumping around so much that the binoculars didn't do him much good. Through the binoculars, I could clearly see a cut on Hagler's face.

In the excitement of the bout, another man came bounding alongside me wanting to look through my binoculars. It turned out to be Marvin Hagler's personal physician. He was wound up tighter than a $2 watch! I lent him my binoculars and he studied the cut on Marvin's face and declared to me in an excited voice, "I've got this, I've got this! It's a cut on his forehead. I can fix it!" He then literally tossed the binoculars over his shoulder in my direction as he ran for Hagler's corner just as the bell rung ending the first round.

The crowd was a continuous deafening roar through the entire fight, which I'm sure was heard not only throughout the entire casino but up and down the entire Las Vegas strip!

During the second round, the exchange between the prize fighters intensified even more, which I didn't think was possible, and the crowd intensified along with them! People were jumping up and down on the bleachers behind me, and the VIPs around me were going nuts with champagne and food were being spilled. At the beginning of the evening, Paul and I had placed our ambulance gurney behind our "Blue" seats and under the "Pink" seat bleachers. Not a great idea. It was completely soiled with food and drink by the end of the evening.

While it was hard to take my eyes off the match, part of my job was to watch the crowd. I watched the movie star Ernie Hudson, who was five seats away from me. I thought he was going to have a heart attack! You would have thought he was in the boxing ring taking the blows directly from both boxers!

Ernie wasn't the only one animated at this event. At most sporting events, one can quickly determine which team/contestant a fan is rooting for. During this fight, I couldn't tell if the fans even knew who they wanted to win. They were cheering on both fighters equally.

The referee ended the fight in the third round, a total of just eight minutes of fighting, by technical knock-out of Tommy Hearns, declaring Marvin Hagler the Middleweight Champion of the World.

The fight was an experience that I will not forget. I think Paul and I had about the best seats in the house. Not only could we see the event perfectly, all the fighters walked passed us going in and out of the ring. Prize fighters were not the only ones walking passed us. We also had well known movie stars passing us by. Thank God, no spectators were hurt during the main event. I'm positive no one would have noticed them until after the fight was over!

The only patient we cared for was the initial unconscious boxer. After the flight, Paul and I chatted with Dr. Romeo while the crowd cleared. As we talked, I saw Brooke Shields, Bo Derek, and Red Foxx also casually hanging out waiting for the crowd to thin. While Red Foxx played an old guy on the TV series "Sanford and son," he was actually a fairly young guy. The fight had Red pretty excited. I chatted with him for a while. He was a huge boxing fan, and promised to come up and harass Paul and I at the next fight. As Red put it, "You guys get better seats than me anyway!"

Once the crowd had cleared, we packed up our gear and headed back to our ambulance, the substation, and home. It would be quite a while before another fight came along that surpassed the one I had witnessed tonight.

For the next week, it was the only thing people in Las Vegas talked about. From what Paul told me, a lot of money changed hands over that fight.

30 April, 1985

The call volume has started to pick up. We'd gone from around 10 calls per shift to approximately 20. Most of them were 'groid' runs. It got to the point where Paul and I could receive a call and guess to a "T" what was wrong with the patient.

Lately, it felt like all we saw were people complaining of chest colds for two weeks, or "I just don't feel well, so I thought I'd give you guys a call." On most shifts, only two or three calls were really legitimate emergencies. For the most part these were typical medical emergencies, but the other day Dave Duritsa and I received a call for a transient that was pushing his shopping cart down a dimly lit street and was struck by a Volkswagen van at about 15 mph.

As we approached the scene, it was like an obstacle course. The contents of the vagrant's cart were scattered over a full city block. I was driving and pulled up alongside the patient and turned on the ambulances sidelights. Our patient was laying along the side of the road all twisted and not moving. Dave was attending, so he grabbed the jump bag and headed for the patient. I parked the ambulance and grabbed the gurney, MAST trousers and the scoop stretcher. Our patient was in his mid-50s and in a bad shape. His left foot was almost completely amputated from the impact, both his femurs were fractured, and he had roughly eight fractured ribs by our count, but his most critical injury was a depressed skull fracture.

An Engine company staffed with basic Emergency Medical Technicians had been dispatched to the accident and they had absolutely no idea what to do. The minute Dave and I saw this guy, we knew his life was quickly slipping away.

As I approached the patient, Dave gave me the rundown of his injuries. While the guy was still breathing on his own, we figured that probably wouldn't last very long. We doubled our efforts to stabilize him.

We placed him on 100% oxygen and secured his spine using a scoop stretcher and then placed him onto the gurney and into the ambulance. His legs were in such bad shape that we used the MAST trousers as a pneumatic splint to hold them in place. The MAST also helped stabilize his blood pressure, which was starting to drop. We quickly applied the trousers and inflated both legs and abdominal compartments. This helped increase his blood pressure long enough for me to get a large bore IV started. I then hopped into the driver's seat and started for the hospital, Code 3.

Since his left foot was nearly amputated, and a lot of vessels were exposed, the increased blood pressure from the MAST trousers caused the extremity to start bleeding again. To remedy this, Dave let out some of the air in the left leg compartment, unwrapped the left leg from the MAST trousers and applied a trauma dressing with a couple of 8 x 10 bandages and then re-inflated the trouser. This worked extremely well to control the leg bleeding, but his extensive internal injuries were beginning to take their toll.

Our patient, already unconscious, stopped breathing. Dave quickly intubated him while we were en route to the hospital. We arrived at the hospital ER and turned the care over to the emergency room staff. They were extremely impressed. From the time we arrived on scene until the time we handed him over to the ER staff only fifteen minutes had elapsed. Seven of those minutes were transport time. Sadly, our patient died in surgery due to a shattered liver and a tear in his descending aorta. The guy could have been struck and landed on the surgeon's operating table and not have survived his injuries.

I really felt sorry for the guy that hit him. He didn't even see the old guy until he was right on top of him, and then there was nothing he could do. When we left for our next call, the driver was still talking to a psychiatrist. I don't know how well he's going to cope when he learns that the fella died.

1 May, 1985

I've had several extremely strange calls. The strangest call occurred yesterday. Paul and I received a request to respond to an automobile accident on I-15, about 20 miles south of town. We arrived on scene to find a 19-year-old Asian male sitting in the back of a Nevada State Troopers squad car. The trooper told me that he could not find anything wrong with the vehicle, and as far as he could tell the young man just drove the vehicle off the road and into the desert. All the trooper knew was that the guy was acting really weird. I said, "Okay, let me talk to this guy and see what's going on." So the trooper let the guy out of the back of the squad car and pointed to me saying, "That guy right there is a paramedic and he's going to check you out."

The young man walked over and stood in front of me. I said, "How are you feeling?" He said, "Can I ask you a question?" I said, "Sure, go ahead." He said, "Do we die?" I said, "Excuse me?" He said, "Do we die?" I said, "Eventually, we all die." He said, "Yes, I suppose so. Well, if you don't need me anymore, I'll be on my way." He started to turn and walk away from me when I caught his shoulder and said, "Wait a minute partner, I want to ask you a few questions as well."

He turned back around and stood at attention in front of me and said, "Yes, Sir!" I said, "Were you in the Army?" He shouted, "Yes, Sir!!" I said "How long?" He replied, "Up until a couple of days ago, Sir!" I said, "Oh... Were you injured at all when your car ran off the road?" He replied, "No, Sir!"

His "Yes, Sir", "No, Sir" stuff was starting to irritate me. So I said,

"Look, just answer my questions with a simple yes or no and you can loosen up a little. But don't move." I looked over at Paul, who was talking to the trooper and gave me a befuddled look. I shrugged my shoulders and said to the state trooper, "He's not physically injured, but his noodle sure is scrambled. Is the Army still using nerve gas?" Paul and the trooper just chuckled.

I looked back to the patient and asked, "What's your name partner?" The young man answered, "Sim." I said, "Sim, I'm going to take you into town and have a doctor look at you."

Sim followed me around to the back of the ambulance, climbed in and laid down on the gurney. I jumped in behind him and locked the door (just in case he decided he didn't want to stay for the ride). For the first few minutes of the ride to the hospital, Sim just sat there staring into space. I sat on the bench beside him trying to get my paperwork done.

I started asking Sim where he lived. I asked, "Sim, what's your home address?" He answered, "Everywhere." I said, "Everywhere? Well where do you get your mail delivered to?" He said, "I don't get mail. I was killed. You know that when I woke up, I found out that I'm God and so now I live everywhere." I said, "Oh... That's... Interesting. So... God... Do you have any relatives that live in Las Vegas?" He said, "I have a cousin." This was starting to become more than I could handle. As my face turned red, tears of laughter began to pool in my eyes. I asked, "And what is this cousin's name? Expecting to hear something like 'Ho Lee Ghost'." I was disappointed when he said, "Martha Lee" and gave a North Las Vegas address.

Sim then became quiet again and stared off into nowhere. I returned to my paperwork when all of a sudden Sim looked at me with a wide-eyed expression and said, "Give me your money!" I looked over at him in annoyance and said, "What?" Sim again reiterated, "Give me your money!" I said, "Why?" Sim replied, "Somebody's got to pay for me." I said, "Pay for what?" Sim said, "I'm an entertainer." I said, "An entertainer is it? What do you do?" He looked at me kind of puzzled and said, "I'm an actor?" I said, "You act?" He said, "No." I said, "How about a singer." Sim lit up and said, "Yeah, a singer! That's what I am!" I said, "Do you know any songs?" Sim said, "I sure do! How about 'Las Vegas'!" And he started singing "Las Vegas, Las Vegas, la de da Las Vegas." Which kind of trailed off into nothing and again Sam was quiet.

Thirty seconds later, he glanced over at me and said, "9 o'clock." I said, "What?" Sim said, "9 o'clock. That's the best time. 9 o'clock." I said, "Okay." Sim asked, "What time is it." I looked at my watch and said, "11:10". Sim said, "Good. We have plenty of time, for time is plenty, and that we have plenty of." I just shook my head and said, "Sounds good to me Sim." Sim then started to fidget a little on the gurney and said, "You know they can't keep us forever." I said, "Sim, you're getting yourself all worked up over nothing." He looked at me with a start, and said, "Nothing?! Nothing is everything and everything is what we have plenty of, and plenty of nothing is more than the time that we were wasting, so they can't hold us forever!!" I said, "Ahh....That's easy for you to say!" To which Sim replied, "9 o'clock, that's the best time, 9 o'clock."

By this point we were six miles from the hospital. Sim then looked over at me as I was finishing my paperwork and said, "Take it off!" I closed my notebook and looked at him with a heavy sigh and said, "What now Sim?" Sim repeated, "Take it off. Your mask. Take it off." Now I may not be the best looking guy around, but no one has ever declared my ugly mug to be a mask! I said, "Sim, I know this will shock to you, but I was born with this face! It's not a mask!" Sim said, "Sure it is! Let me help you take it off." He then lurched from the gurney and tried to grab, or should I say claw, at my face.

I seized both his wrists and said firmly, "Sim! Let's get one thing perfectly clear. You don't touch me! At all!! Got it!? If you try a stunt like that again, I'll tie you down to my gurney!" I then firmly pressed him back onto the ambulance gurney and held him there for a second. When I let go, Sim sat pouting to himself, but he didn't move.

His attention span was extremely short and before long the whole episode was forgotten and I was his best buddy all over again. Sim continued to spout off inappropriate sentences the rest of the way to the hospital. He was like a small child with attention deficit disorder. While trying to get my paperwork written, every time I looked up, Sim was getting into something. I'd yell at him and say, "Sim! No! You put that down and just sit there! And don't touch anything!"

Finally, after what felt like an eternity, we arrived at the hospital. I jumped out of the back of the ambulance and said, "Sim. Follow me." Sim immediately jumped out of the ambulance and started walking in the wrong direction. I grumbled, "I can't handle this anymore." I chased after him and grabbed him by the hand, and led him into the emergency room and sat him down on a stool. He immediately picked up a urine sample that was sitting on the counter in front of him and started fiddling with it. I said, "Sim! Put that down! Turn around and don't touch anything!"

A nurse came by and I gave her my report on Sim and we led him to a room and sat him on the bed. The nurse started to walk away, leaving Sim unattended. I rushed to catch up with the nurse and said, "Look, someone is going to have to stay with this guy, otherwise he'll be wandering all over the emergency room. I had no sooner finished saying this, when I turned around and Sim was messing with medical supplies on a shelf in the exam room. I shook my head, walked back over to Sim, led him back to his bed, held up the palm of my hand and said, "Stay."

The nurse looked at me and said, "I see what you mean! I'll get security." As the nurse was reaching for the phone, Sim jumped off the bed, grabbed my wrist and said, "Let's make a break for it!

They're not looking!" I said, "No Sim, you've got to stay in the bed." But it was too late. Sim was already starting to run down the hall. I thought to myself, "I can't believe this shit." I took off after him, tackled him in the hall and dragged him back to his room. By this time security was there. Sim was put into soft restraints and secured to the bed.

I had finished my paperwork and was having a friendly conversation with several of the ER staff members when I heard a screech from the hall in front of Sim's exam room. I thought to myself, *What now!*

Sim had gotten loose from his restraints and had snuck out of the exam room, grabbed a cleaning lady and gave her a big kiss. He then ran out the side door of the emergency room. I just shook my head and said to the emergency room nurse, "He's aaaall yours."

The rest of that shift was mellow, with only a few calls to the casinos, and then nothing the rest of the shift.

5 May, 1985

My days off were filled with volunteer work. I was either delivering a lecture for Mercy ambulance, helping with a charity, or teaching at the community college (a paid gig). I had also been able to pick up a few flights on a local air ambulance service.

With all the work, I still managed pick up a new hobby. That new hobby was scuba diving. I thought that an old eardrum injury would have prevented me from enjoying this hobby, but after having a couple ER doctors examine my ears, I was given the green light to give the hobby a try.

Terry Kozlowski and I signed up for the scuba diving course together. To be Scuba certified, one needed to attend 12 two-hour lectures, which we completed over a two-week period.

The lectures included both classroom and in-pool instruction. By the fourth in-pool session, I was totally comfortable in the water. I didn't have any problem equalizing my middle ear pressures like I thought I would. Everything was a piece of cake. Unfortunately, Terry had a bit more trouble getting used to the water and equalizing her middle ear. She was initially scared of the equipment and was constantly trying to hold her breath underwater instead of breathing normally. But she was a real trooper and by the last class was just as comfortable in the water as I was. The course cost $150 and at the end of two weeks, we were certified by "Scuba Schools International", given access to all the dive club's equipment, and given a three-day, two-tonight scuba diving package on Catalina Island, just off the California coast, near Los Angeles.

I couldn't wait to scheduled our trip to Catalina and try out my new skills. An EMT friend named Rick Kohl was also a scuba diving enthusiast and invited me to join him on a dive-weekend at Lake Mead. Rick was a former Navy seal, and a world-class diver. He took pity on me and showed me the ropes on how to improve my scuba diving technique.

I loved diving at Lake Mead. The water was warm, clear, and although there really wasn't that much to see, I loved the new found freedom of floating under water. On subsequent dives at Lake Mead, Rick introduced me to two locations where local dive clubs had sunk boats. These boats sat in about 50 to 60 feet of water and were big enough that you could swim through them. Scuba diving is like being in another world, and in that underwater world, you can fly!

9 May,1985

My lectures were starting to get noticed by people outside the Clark County High School community. I was asked to be a guest speaker at the "Insurance Women of Las Vegas" public awareness program on teenage drunk driving. There were several prominent city figures present. The mayor of Las Vegas, all the TV stations, two local newspapers, the predominant insurance carriers in the area, and the main municipal court judges. I was one of ten speakers that spoke to this group. When the program was over, many from the group came up to congratulate me on my informative lecture. Several took my name and telephone number to speak at future lectures.

One person that sat in on my lecture was Terry's step-father, Mike Parenti, Vice President of the Southwest Region for Pepsi-Cola. Mike later contacted me and asked if I was interested in working for him. He offered me a starting salary of $25,000 a year with the opportunity to move up into a district manager's position within a year. The opportunities and benefits he listed were more than I could resist, so I applied, and went for an interview. Mr. Parenti and I hit it off right from the beginning. He asked me a few basic questions about my work experience and what I thought of the idea of working for Pepsi-Cola. He then shifted to a conversation about who he should invite to a big party he was going to be throwing in a couple of weeks, and what I thought about different catering services.

The whole interview was nothing like I had expected. Mike said, "Thanks for coming in. I'll give you a call after I finish interviewing the rest of the candidates."

While I didn't get the job. I was extremely grateful for the opportunity to interview and that Mike thought of me for the position at all. Terry told me that I was second on the list, but was beaten out by a gentleman that already worked for Pepsi and was a supervisor from a different plant.

Work continued to have moments of complete insanity. The Las Vegas summer activities had gotten underway, and every shift was busier than the one before. For mid-May, the weather was extremely warm, and there hasn't been a drop of rain for the entire year. My schedule had also been crazy as usual. I went to work at 8 AM, for a 24-hour shift, which typically turned into a 26 or 27-hour shift. I tried to get a few hours of household chores done before heading out in the afternoon for scuba classes or a high school lecture somewhere in town.

It hadn't even dawned on me that my birthday was just a couple days away. I was so preoccupied with work, lectures, and scuba diving classes that I imagined the day coming and going without much fanfare. My roommate, Robin, and on-again, off-again girlfriend, Terry, however had other plans. They thought it should be properly celebrated, and they began to plan a huge surprise birthday party for me. No easy task!

First off, they should have asked me if I could fit it into my schedule. Secondly, they should have booked me into something else so that I didn't fill up my schedule on my own. The surprise party was planned for May 11, five days before my actual birthday. I thought it very strange that every time I tried to schedule an event, or offered to work a shift, it was either flat-out denied, or initially accepted, only to be later declined.

Eventually, I was told that I was needed to discuss a few projects involving auto safety, local high schools, and Mercy ambulance. The pitch, was that I was to be the public spokesman for Mercy ambulance. It all sounded completely legitimate since I had pretty much been doing this already. I just figured that Mercy ambulance wanted to formalize my project. A luncheon date was set to get me out of the house, so that Robin could set up for the party.

Unfortunately, they hadn't planned far enough ahead. I lived on such a tight schedule, that I figured the average luncheon meeting would only last between one and a half to two hours, and I had already scheduled myself to help with a "summer safety overnighter" program for 150 - 6 to 10-year-olds. The event was to start at 6 PM that night. Long story short, the party had to be called off and everyone was upset with me. I couldn't figure out why until the "big plot" was finally revealed to me. It was then my turn to laugh. I said, "With my schedule? You would have had to ask me for a date a month in advance, and maybe I could have taken it off." But I appreciated the thought and felt bad to have missed the party.

While the summer safety overnighter was fun, I would have preferred to have gone to my surprise party. Those kids drove me nuts. We didn't have nearly enough chaperones for a group that size. They kept me up all night just keeping them in the designated areas, and preventing them from killing each other! They reminded me of Sim!

I was so tired the next morning (May 12) when I headed for work that I prayed we'd have a slow morning and that I could get a little sleep. No such luck. We received our first call the second we went in-service, and it was two in the afternoon before we returned to the substation. I felt like a zombie. The numbness had not only spread from between my eyes and to my whole head, but also to my whole body! I couldn't tell you what the calls were that we ran that morning and afternoon.

I headed home at 8:30 the next morning more exhausted than I think I had ever been. I collapsed onto my bed, still in my work clothes and slept until noon when Terry came to the house and woke me for our scuba diving classes. I was still dead tired, but figured I should get up and do something useful.

After a two hour swim, I figured that was about all the usefulness I had left in me. I returned home and went straight back to sleep, and slept through the night until my alarm clock sounded to rise and shine for my next work day.

The end of May was upon me, I couldn't believe how fast the year was passing. A friend from my hometown, Kingsley, Iowa, had been writing letters to me over the past few months.

Blake "Gomer" Laddusaw, was keenly interested in following my footsteps to Las Vegas and working as an Emergency Medical Technician (EMT). Blake had passed his National Registry EMT exam and was volunteering on the local ambulance squad, just like I had a few years before. He was hoping to make Emergency Medical Services (EMS) his chosen profession.

After months of communications, he finally booked a trip to Las Vegas and I helped him schedule an interview with Mercy ambulance. Sadly, the middle management team at Mercy was having a severe case of "Head-Up-Butt syndrome", and informed me two days prior to Blake's arrival, that policies had changed and that they were not going to interview anyone until the end of June, a full month away. I was hot! I said, "Now wait a second, I told you that Blake was coming down specifically for this interview a month ago, and now, all of a sudden you decide to change your policy? Two days before he arrives? And not even talk to him?!" They replied, "Well…, well…, we'll talk to him, but we won't consider hiring him." I was steamed! I said, "Well that's really cute! This guy is spending his own money to fly 1500 miles out here for an interview that you already agreed to and you won't even consider hiring him? Have you ever thought that this might be a reason why recruitment is having such difficulty hiring folks?" As expected, management's sluffed off my statements as, "He's just overreacting because Blake's a friend from home."

Sadly, Mercy's management had the opinion that they didn't have to do anything to recruit new employees because they were the only game in town, and that the limelight of Las Vegas would do all the recruiting for them. Yes, the lights of Las Vegas did attract paramedics, but not necessarily the best paramedics. In reality, the best paramedics only worked for a couple years and then moved on, leaving middle management shocked that they would leave such a plum job.

Lately, the attitude around Mercy could have been classified in a word, "tense." Everyone was unhappy. The majority were looking for work elsewhere.

Oh, there were still a few that swore by Mercy ambulance "lock, stock and barrel," but I think they were few and feared that they couldn't get work anyplace else.

As of 1 June, 1985, Mercy was ten paramedics short. That shortage placed a tremendous strain on the remaining paramedics to cover all the shifts. I have to admit that I'd taken on the attitude of, "just let me do my job and leave me alone." Don't get me wrong, I loved being a paramedic, but I didn't enjoy working for a company that did nothing but exploit my talents.

For example, at the end of May, the American Ambulance Association Convention was held at the MGM Grand hotel. For weeks, Mercy management had been asking EMTs and paramedics to help man the company booth and support the Ambulance Association. Finally, a day before the convention was to open, enough people were coerced into "volunteering" in order to adequately support the event. The convention went off without a hitch, and everyone was thoroughly impressed with Mercy ambulance throughout the convention.

During the final day of the convention, a large party was thrown for everyone that orchestrated the event. Our boss, Bob Forbus, Executive Manager of Mercy ambulance, was given a large plaque for <u>his</u> efforts. Bob stood up and gave this long-winded bull shit speech and didn't even acknowledge the fact that the EMTs and paramedics present were volunteering at the convention in addition to working their regular 24 hour shifts. That just pissed me off, but to really kick the situation in the ass, Bob decided to pay the office secretaries for working the event but refused to pay the EMTs and paramedics. Adding insult to injury, it was leaked that the large hospitality party sponsored by Mercy ambulance came out of the Mercy ambulance employee welfare fund, and Mercy employees were not even invited to the damn thing!

That was it. It was more than I or anyone else could stand. The mass exodus from Mercy had begun. Over the next two weeks, one third of all Mercy paramedics had put in applications to other services in Colorado, California, and Texas. Mercy was either blind to what was going on, or didn't care.

Gomer had flown down to Las Vegas and was living with Robin and I, free of charge, while he waited for Mercy to decide if they were going to hire him. He had volunteered to help Mercy at the convention in the hope that his good work would help him get hired. He didn't even get a thank you from the company. While all this was going on, the streets of Las Vegas were going wild.

There was a major accident at the corner of Sahara Boulevard and Boulder Highway in which a van ran a red light and struck a car. The driver of the van was extremely intoxicated and was transporting four other people with him. The impact with the car resulted in the van rolling three times. Three of the four passengers in the van were killed. Two of those killed were the intoxicated driver's brothers, whom he had to climb over to get out of the van. The driver in the car he hit was also killed instantly. It was estimated that the van was traveling at about 70 miles an hour and literally drove over the top of the car.

I personally wasn't on the call, but I heard it was a gruesome scene. The driver of the van was arrested on four counts of vehicular homicide and one count of felony D.U.I., which is a 10 to 15 year prison sentence, with at least five years served before he could even be eligible for parole.

3 June, 1985

Paul Young was still my regular work partner. I think he went into D.T's (delirium tremens – what happens to drunks when they withdraw) anytime he had to work with someone else.

I was very happy for him. It looked very likely that he would get into medical school that fall or early next spring. He had an interview at a medical school in Ames, Iowa. I laughed and told him, "The winters are pretty cold up there you know." He laughed and said, "I'd go to Nome, Alaska if they had a medical school and would accept me!" I continued to tease him about living in Iowa and the fact that I didn't think he could handle the -30°F winters or the 100% humidity summers. He would respond with something like, "Anything would be better than having to put up with you for another year."

Most of the calls that Paul and I had respond to had been anti-climactic. I don't know if it's because Paul and I work so smoothly together or if it's because we just became desensitized, so nothing seemed that tremendous.

One call that sticks out in my mind was to the Tropicana hotel for a possible fall. Upon our arrival, we found an elderly woman lying face-down at the base of the long flight of stairs. The Tropicana hotel security guards were standing around, not doing anything other than keeping other tourists from getting in the way. As Paul and I approached the scene, everyone was acting as though the woman was dead. So I walked up to the first security guard and asked him, "Is she dead?" He whispered back, "I don't know." I asked, "Has anyone checked for a pulse?" The security guard looked a little flustered and looked over to the other security guard and whispered, "Hey Jim. Does she have a pulse?" I didn't even wait for an answer. I brushed past the two guards mumbling, "incompetent damn…"

As I began to assess the elderly woman, I noted that her lips were cyanotic (blue) and that her respirations were extremely shallow and irregular. She had a faint pulse at about 114 bpm, and was completely unresponsive to deep painful stimuli. There was a large hematoma (bump) above the left eye and forehead due to striking the floor at the base of the stairs. There were several other areas of swelling along the side and back of her skull. A witness reported that she had tripped at the top of the stairs and went head over heels all the way down to the base.

Paul checked her pupils and noted that they were mid-range and non-reactive. No one knew her and we could find no medical information in her purse. We started an IV and intubated her to protect her airway. We applied the ECG monitor and noted a normal sinus, tachycardia rhythm. We then placed her on to a scoop stretcher for spinal mobilization and urgently transported her to the hospital. A few hours later, I inquired at the hospital as to how she was doing. She was just coming back from the CT scanner, still unconscious, and completely dependent on a ventilator. Her CT revealed a skull fracture and a subarachnoid bleed. She also suffered several small bleeds in the deep core of her brain. The neurologist didn't think she would ever regained consciousness, and if she did her recovery would be only slight. How sad. It reminded me how fragile and fleeting life can be.

While the city is always home to "crazies", it appeared as though the crazies were hosting their own convention! I swear that every other patient Paul and I transported this past week had a mental health condition. We were not the only crew experiencing the same situation.

Paul and I had just dropped off a patient at the Southern Nevada Memorial hospital emergency room when another crew arrived in the ER with a white gentleman that had shaved his head and painted his whole body black with black shoe polish and was singing Elvis Presley songs and attempting to imitate Elvis's voice.

As they wheeled him past us, I said, "Oh, I have to go watch this!" The transporting crew transferred him to the hospital gurney and attempted to help the ER staff strap him down. He was going berserk and yelling at everyone.

Sometimes "crazies" just bring out the worst in me. I walked into the room as seven people were trying to strap this guy down. I walked to the head of the bed as the guy was screaming, "Go on then! Kill me! See if I care!" I calmly looked at him and replied,

"We don't need to kill you. You're already dead." He suddenly calmed and stopped struggling to think about what I had just told him. Unfortunately, he then lost focus and returned to screaming and hollering at everyone else. Eventually he would refocus his rage on me and say, "You think you're pretty tough, tying me down like this don't you?" I innocently replied, "No, not really. I tie my dog up like this all the time and he never thinks I'm tough."

Once again, my response would catch him off guard and cause him to quiet down to think for a minute. You could almost see the demons in his mind working to regain control of the conversation. A minute later he would become agitated again and say, "Oh yeah? Well I think you're pretty tough." And I'd say, "Well, you ought too." And then he'd say, "I ought to what?" I'd say, "Think that I'm pretty tough." This again would confuse him for a moment and then he'd say, "But I don't think you're tough." I just smiled and said, "But who's tied up right now." This would bring him right back to the beginning of the conversation and he'd say, "So go ahead. Kill me! See if I care!" to which I again replied, "But you're already dead, don't you know that Elvis died almost ten years ago?"

By this point "Elvis" was securely tied to the bed and no longer a threat to himself or others. He settled back into regaling the emergency department with his Elvis impersonation and songs. I clasped my hands together, addressed the ER staff stating, "Well my work here is done." And returned to the reception desk to see if Paul was ready to depart. It was comical watching people walk through the emergency room. They would hear "Elvis" singing in the side room and wonder what in the world was going on.

Paul and I were just leaving the emergency room when we heard a large crash back in "Elvis'" room. We quickly ran to the room to find good old "Elvis" in the middle of the room, still tied down but rolling about freely. It appears that he had managed to get the brake on the gurney to release and was using it like a bumper car. He had pretty much destroyed everything in the room. The ER guards and nursing staff just shook their heads and closed the door saying, "Well at least he can't break anything else." I shook my head and walked away to the sound of "Elvis" singing his songs and bouncing off the walls in room #3.

The "crazy convention" was still in full swing as Paul and I responded on our very next call. It was to an apartment complex for a gentleman dancing around the community pool, singing and doing his rendition of martial arts poses. I shook my head as I walked into the pool area.

Several police officers had gathered off to the side of the pool. As we walked up to them, I said, "Well, go get 'em guys." They said, "We already tried that. Every time we get near him, he jumps into the pool!" I said, "Oh, then you guys don't need us, you need water rescue!"

Paul then leaned next to my ear and whispered, "Pssst, we *are* water rescue." I whispered back, "I know that and you know that, but these guys don't know that!" The police officers advised that they were going to wait for a couple more officers to arrive, and then storm the pool area. The guy was big and they were worried that he just might know martial arts. I was still in rare form from "Elvis" back in the ER that I quipped, "Oh.., sort of like a human version of bobbing for apples!" I thought it was hilarious, but the police officers didn't quite see the humor.

Taking my cue from their stern looks, I cleared my throat and redirected, "Are there any family members around?" One of the officers pointed to an elderly couple and said, "They are his parents, but they don't want to get involved." As I started walking to the couple I replied, "Seriously?" I spoke briefly to the elderly couple, and it was quite clear that their son had significant mental health problems that were beyond their ability to control.

I then walked over to the side of the pool where this guy was chanting and going through his bizarre poses. I said, "Sir?" No answer. "Sir?" Still no answer. I looked over at his parents, who were both trying hard not to be noticed (especially by the neighbors.) I said, "Excuse me, yes you two, can you tell me what your son's name is." They both turned white as a sheet and scurried off to their apartment. I yelled after them, "If you have to go home to look it up, well then never mind." I then looked over at the gathering crowd and asked, "Does anyone know this guy's name?" Out of the peanut gallery I heard someone yell "John." I replied, "Thank you!" And the crowd replied in a chorus, "You're welcome!" (Apparently this was where the participants of the "crazy convention" were all staying!) I shook my head and looked back at the guy dancing around the pool and thought, "and the police think *this* guy is crazy!"

I then walked to the pool fence nearest "John" and casually asked, "John, can you come over here for a second? I need to talk to you." To my surprise, John stopped his chanting and walked to the gates, opened it, and walked over to where I was standing. He stood about 6'2" tall and was in extremely good physical shape. He politely asked, "What can I do for you?" I extended my hand and said, "Hi. My name is Ty. I'm a paramedic. I was called here because your neighbors think you're crazy. John then turned and looked at the crowd of people and said, "My neighbors all think I'm crazy?" To this, the crowd all started shaking their heads, "No" and stepping backwards. "That's right, John," I replied.

John shook his head and said, "They're all sick in the minds." At this point the crowd suddenly decided they all had better things to do and quickly vacated the area. I said, "I know that John, but I need you to go to the hospital with me and have a doctor prove them all wrong." John looked around for the second time and then said, "Okay".

By this time, the police department had mustered the "7th Brigade" and were marching across the courtyard towards John and me. John looked over at them and said, "What's with those guys?" I said, "I don't know. I think they are after parking ticket violators." John shrugged his shoulders and said, "Oh". The astonished looking police officers as the row parted in the middle and John and I walked to the ambulance. John jumped inside and we headed off for the hospital. Paul slid into the driver seat of the ambulance chuckling to himself saying, "I'm impressed Ty, I'm really impressed!"

John rested on the ambulance gurney and I grabbed my medical clipboard and tried to ask John a few basic questions about himself.

"John," I asked. "What's your apartment number." John responded, "6" and then start humming. I thought to myself "Great. John is going to start flipping out and I'm in the back with him all by myself, and he's not even the least bit restrained." I smiled and politely asked, "John. What's your birthday?" John told me, but kept on humming. I wrote it down and said, "Okay, now John do you have any past medical problems that I should be aware of? Like cancer… or heart problems… or diabetes… or seizures…. or mental health problems…..?" I was afraid that the "mental health problems" might get him going again, but he hadn't even heard me. He was off in his own little world before I had even finished asking the question. His humming had now turned into a bounce and the bounce was on its way towards a dance.

John was now dancing in the back of my ambulance chanting, "Hummm, Hawwww, Hooo, Yeaaa, Doe, Rae, Meee, Faaa, Soooo, Laaa." Then, out of nowhere, John broke into full "Sound of Music" mode! He started singing and dancing, "Doe, a deer, a female deer; Rae, lock of golden sun; Me, a name I call myself……" Paul was barely able to keep the ambulance on the road, and I was not sure whether to laugh or be terrified.

But John kept on singing undaunted. I figured I'd better get John's mind on something else before he started singing, "the Hills are alive with the sound of music!"

I said, "John. John! Where did you learn your judo?" John suddenly stop singing and looked at me and said, "It's not judo! It's Jujitsu!" I said, "Oh! Where did you learn your jujitsu?" He said, "I didn't learn it. I just know it." I said "Oh. So did you ever spend any time in the military?" John said, "Yeah, I spent some time in 'Nam'." I said, "Oh really? Where were you posted?" John replied "All over the place. Long Sang Che and My Sow Pen, and all them places." I replied, "Very interesting. You know John, I've studied martial arts as well." John continued to be distracted by our conversation and replied, "Oh? What form?" I said, "The art of Do Run Fast!" John looked puzzled for a moment and said, "I've never heard of that form. It must be a Western Hemisphere branch." I said, "No. It's pretty universal and international."

At this point, John had lost interest in our conversation and returned to his chanting and dancing around the back of the ambulance, but the distraction had worked and John had forgotten all about the sound of music and was now doing his rendition of "The King and I".

John sang and hummed all the way to the hospital, but once at the hospital, he settled right down and walked in with us without any fuss or fight. I thought we might have a bit of trouble when John asked whether we were going to give him a ride home, but Paul was on the ball and said, "Gee John, we sure would like to, but golly, we have to get back out onto the street so we can save more lives." John relaxed and said, "I suppose so. Well, thanks for the lift guys." John waved and we waved back. The ER nurse smiled and waved as well. I patted the nurse on the shoulder as I exited and said, "Introduce John to "Elvis," they'd make quite a duo."

As we were walking out to our ambulance, Ron Barnes was walking a completely naked man into the ER. I glanced over to Paul and said, "We can't go, I have to know this guy's story."

Ron had a tight grip on the arm of the naked man whose demeanor was beyond euphoric. He was happy to see everyone and was bouncing around like a little puppy. When I say he was "happy", every part of his naked body, especially his male anatomy was very "happy." He was jumping around claiming to be 'Superman". One of the ER nurses saw him coming through the ambulance bay doors and yelled at Ron, "I don't need to see that shit! Wrap a sheet around him!!!"

Ron lead the now "sheet-wrapped, erotically charged, Superman" into the crazy corner. As the ER nurses and security guards struggled to secure Naked Superman to the bed, he kept fighting and saying, "I'm Superman, your restraints can't hold me! Ron didn't miss a beat, he leaned passed the ER staff holding up a pen light and said, "Hey Superman, do you know what this is? It's a Kryptonite beam!" With that, he turned it on and shined the light into his eyes. Superman screamed and fell limp as a rag onto the bed. Ron handed the pen light to the ER guard and said, "With my compliments."

With "Superman" secured in the room with "Elvis" and John, I said, "Ok, Ron. Out with it. What is 'Naked Man's' story. Ron related that they had been called to Fremont street for this guy. Dispatch had received reports of this guy running up and down the street, naked as the day he was born, masturbating. The Metro police had been called and were starting to get him corralled just as Ron and his partner arrived on the scene. Just as Metro thought they had him apprehended, he squatted down and shit a huge turd, which he then picked up and began to eat! Laughing and just as happy as could be. I said incredulously, "You are making this up!"

Ron laughed and said, "It gets better! When the Metro Officers saw him do this, they were done. No one wanted to touch him!

Ron related that he then opened the side door of the ambulance and shouted to the naked crazy man. "HEY YOU!!" When "Naked Superman" turned to look at him, Ron then said, *"Wipe that shit-*

eating-grin off your face and get into my ambulance!"

I don't think I stopped laughing for the rest of the shift!

The call volume continued to increase over the summer months. Each month, Mercy broke the previous month's record for the number of emergency calls ran. The first week of June, Mercy ambulance responded to over 700 emergency calls. That number didn't include non-emergent calls or scheduled transfers. Just the emergency, 911, lights and siren calls.

I was exhausted and ready for a break.

7 June 1985

Terry Kozlowski and I had been planning to take our final open water scuba diving test on Catalina Island for weeks. Catalina Island is located just off the coast of Los Angeles, California. Our scuba diving course fees included a three-day and two-night accommodation on Catalina Island, with three days of open water scuba diving.

I had my fill of Las Vegas and was so eager to get away. We booked an entire week on Catalina Island. I was excited to be off for a whole week doing nothing but swimming, scuba diving, and baking in the sun on the beach!

Everything was set, until a week before we were to leave. At that time, Terry told me she couldn't get the whole week off. My first reaction was anger. Then it was one of curiosity. How was she going to get back to Las Vegas because I sure wasn't going to go back early!

After the initial news broke, my anger subsided and I finally accepted the fact that I would have to come home two days earlier. I just figured I'd go down to Lake Mead and layout on the beach there.

But, of course, two days before my vacation was to start, Mercy ambulance tried to tell me I was required to attend a mandatory meeting on the third day of my vacation. When Mike Sherwood told me this, I just laughed in his face saying, "You've got two chances of me showing up, slim and none!"

8 June, 1985

On the morning of my vacation, I ended my shift at 8 AM, sped home at lightning speed to change clothes and load the car for the trip. I knew what I wanted to take, so it only took me 15 minutes to pack and I was out the door and over to Terry's house.

Now, it must be bred into a female's nature to take 50 times longer to pack the same amount of stuff. So there I sat, and sat, I pondered going home and hoping that she would be ready by tomorrow morning. I also thought about ordering a pizza or something else while I waited. But, through intense training and the patience of Job, I managed not to lose my temper and we were on our way by 12:30. This should have been an omen, but no, I was too ignorant to see the signs. I was happy to be getting out of town and felt I could put up with anything as long as my car was moving further and further away.

I loved the warm air as we flew across the desert floor between Baker and Barstow, California. I had the windows down and the stereo blaring. I was in heaven. Terry wasn't so enthusiastic, but life's a bitch and then you die! This was my vacation and I was going to enjoy. After months and months of ambulance work, I needed to tend to my needs.

We arrived at the San Pedro pier in the Los Angeles Harbor, just in time to catch the 6 PM ferry to Catalina Island. The ferry pulled into Avalon Harbor on Catalina Island at 8 PM. We had made reservations at the Catherine hotel, which was only a couple of blocks from the Avalon pier.

After dropping our belongings off in our room, we headed down to the lounge to listen to a live band play. I couldn't believe it, the band was a local band from Las Vegas.

Unbelievable! Here I was, a 1000 miles from Las Vegas, trying to forget the place and here was one of their local bands! Well, at least they were a good. We ate, drank, and danced the night away, finally falling asleep at 3 AM.

The next morning, we headed to Casino Point to go diving. I was eager to get into the water. Bill, our dive instructor, explained where we were going to go and then we put on our gear and headed for the water. I was ready to get wet.

With gear in place, I jumped in to the bay and started swimming down. It was phenomenal! The colors were spectacular with beautiful fish and coral everywhere. Thousands of them, and all different shapes and colors. I was so enamored with this new environment that I had almost forgotten about Terry and Bill. I looked around, but couldn't find them. I returned to the surface and found Bill and Terry still at the water's edge.

Terry wasn't taking to the water as easily as I had. The water in the pool had been calm. In the ocean, the waves were completely freaking her out. She finally managed to leave the shoreline and slip below the surface of the water. We followed Bill down, down and down. Traveling through spectacular kelp forests and coral. This was a world I never knew existed. I saw hundreds of different schools of fish and sea life on the floor of the ocean. We swam down to 60 feet of water and into an old freighter that had sunk some years before in a storm. The water was a lot colder and the colors not as bright, due to less light, but everything was just as interesting.

We swam into the cargo port of the sunken ship. While many divers had swam this ship before us, it was still intact and very interesting, although a little spooky. Everything was upside down. There were even a few pictures still on the walls. There were little air pockets all along the floor which was now the ceiling, and the air pockets would roll back and forth giving you the impression that the bubbles were alive. We swam to the front of the ship and out the hole which had caused the ship's untimely demise.

Once outside the ship, we swam under the full length of the wreckage and came back up towards the shore. While swimming towards the shore, Bill caught a baby shark and tried to hand it to Terry. But Terry had no intentions of messing with something that might remember her, grow up and want to mess with her back. Bill then handed the little shark to me, which I eagerly took hold of like I would a bullhead fish back on the farm. It was about two feet long and completely unimpressed with all of the attention it was getting. I was really surprised that its skin was extremely rough, like sandpaper. He also had plenty of teeth! I was wearing gloves and when I tried to let go of this damn shark, I couldn't get him off my glove. I ended up almost having to throw him off my glove before he came loose, and then once loose he kept following me!

Call me a chicken, but I get kind of paranoid when sharks start following me. I shushed him off and quickly swam away. For my first open-water dive, it was more than I could have hoped for.

Over the next three days, we made another six dives. On one particular dive, I came across a large bat ray. A bat ray is in the manta ray/stingray family. This thing was the largest fish I had ever seen underwater. It was about six feet across and had a torso about three to four feet long, and it just glided through the water without effort. Also during that dive, I came across a small octopus. It looked really neat, but wasted no time finding a hole to hide in.

Our time spent out of the water was relaxing. We basked in the sun or sat out on the patio of the Catherine hotel. I loved listening to the ocean at night. It was extremely relaxing and just what the doctor ordered for getting Las Vegas and all the hustle and bustle out of my system.

It may sound wrong, but the only downfall of the vacation was having Terry alone. She just couldn't understand why, outside of diving, I really didn't want to do anything else. All I wanted to do was relax; and to me relaxing didn't include shopping or jogging through the city, or a 20-mile bike ride. I still managed to enjoy myself, and before I knew it my vacation was over. We loaded our stuff onto the Catalina ferry and an hour later we were back in the car heading for Las Vegas.

It appeared that Mercy's inconsideration for their employees was continuing to grow. My time off did not help my attitude towards the company. Paul was getting ready to go to medical school and I just wasn't sure if I could handle working with anyone else. When I first started working for Mercy ambulance, I saw a lot of promise and potential for promotion. But as time passed, I'd seen less promotion and less promise for a long-term professional future there.

In my opinion, the company was starting to regress. Like most of the employees that had been there for more than a year, I knew it was time for me to move on.

Despite my love of emergency medicine, busting my butt on 36 hour shifts for minimum pay was becoming more than I could stand. I also really liked Las Vegas and the desert. The thought of moving to another area of the country really didn't thrill me. I had already placed applications with both the Las Vegas City and Clark County Fire Departments, and while things initially looked promising, a shortfall of about $4 million in the county funds resulted in both the police and fire departments having to pause their hiring for another two years. Two years of the same rigmarole was more than I could muster, I needed to find another option.

10 – NEXT STEPS

26 June, 1985

Over the past two weeks, I had been discussing career options with different paramedics as we worked together. I expressed my frustrations concerning Mercy's administration and the desire to better myself. Paul had encouraged me to take his path, and go back to medical school and study to be a doctor. The thought had intrigued me, but I didn't think I could financially swing it. I would've loved to be an ER Doc, but the thought of being $200,000 in debt didn't appeal to me. I needed to save money first.

Other paramedics had indicated that they were moving to other cities with more stable ambulance administrations. I wasn't ready to leave Las Vegas just yet. Then Rick Acosta jumped into the driver's seat of my ambulance. Over the course of the day, I had the same conversation with him that I had had with a half-dozen other paramedics. Rick offered an alternative that I hadn't considered. The Nevada Nuclear Test Site was hiring paramedics and Rick was going to go fill out an application in the morning after our shift ended.

I knew a little bit about the test site, but not much. I spent the rest of the shift grilling Rick about working at the test site. Rick related that the Nevada Nuclear Test Site (NTSB) is managed by the U.S. Department of Energy (DOE). The main gate is located about 65 miles northwest of the city of Las Vegas but that people that worked there took special buses from town to the test site and back. It was formerly known as the Nevada Proving Grounds, in the 1950's. During that time, they tested above-ground atomic bombs. The Test Site is huge and covers an area of central Nevada that is a bit larger that the state of Rhode Island. The first above-ground test occurred at Frenchman Flat on 27 January, 1951 and was with a 1-kiloton-of-TNT equivalent atomic bomb dropped from the air.

During the 1950s, the mushroom clouds from over 100 tests could be seen as far as 100 miles away. The detonations could also be felt in the city of Las Vegas, and the mushroom clouds could be seen from the tops of downtown hotels.

I exclaimed, "100 atomic bombs! The place should be glowing more than the Las Vegas Strip at night!" Rick said that unlike in the movies, the radioactive 'half-life' from the atomic detonations drops off really fast. "You wouldn't want to go camping on top of one of those places, but working around them exposes you to more radiation from the sun than from the ground."

Rick also informed me that the Nevada Test Site contained 28 different areas, each with its own small town and support buildings in which Test Site Paramedic worked. It also has ten heliports, and two airstrips.

Paramedics hired at the Test Site are not federal employees, but rather employees of the subcontractor Reynolds Electric and Engineering (REECo). Since the Test Site is considered a "Classified Federal Reservation," all employees that work there must undergo an extensive background check to get a government security clearance. Paramedics get what is called a "Black Star 'Q' Clearance" that grants access, on a need to know basis, to all areas of the Test Site.

New paramedics are initially assigned to the main clinic in Mercury, Nevada, which is a small town on the edge of the Test Site that has stores, restaurants, a movie theater, and homes where people live full-time. Paramedics that man aide stations in one of the 28 different areas function similar to "Independent Duty Corpsmen" in the Navy.

The Paramedics also performed "Nuclear Re-entry" duties, meaning that when a nuclear device was detonated, they would support the scientists going in to check their experiment and perform rescue operations if emergences occurred.

The main point that hit home early in the conversation was the fact that they paid $7 an hour *more* than Mercy ambulance. Rick related that most of the bad things I had heard about the test site had come from disgruntled, former employees, in essence, people that had been asked to leave.

Rick had talked to current employees working there and had found that things weren't as they had been portrayed. In fact, the job was probably one of the best places to work as a paramedic in the nation.

In addition to starting paramedics off at $23,000 a year, (not including overtime) they had a retirement plan and excellent health insurance benefits. By the end of the shift, I was sold. I jumped in my car and followed Rick to the REECo. I placed my application that Thursday morning and by the following Wednesday, they were calling me to come in for an interview.

Initially, I didn't think much about the fact that they had gotten back to me so quickly. That is, until I found out that my application had been chosen from over 100 other applications. It made all the dues (volunteer work, public speaking, and a clean work record) worthwhile!

On my next day off work, I went in for my interview and toured the Mercury medical facility. Mercury is a "closed town" in Nye County, Nevada, about five miles north of U.S. Route 95, and 65 miles northwest of Las Vegas. A "closed town" means that it is not accessible to the general public. You needed to have a security clearance to live there, and no children were allowed. It was named after the mercury mines that existed in the general vicinity a hundred years before the town itself was established. It was constructed by the Atomic Energy Commission to house and service the staff of the test site. The specific site was initially known as Jackass Flats, NV.

Mercury had on average, 200 people living there year-round, but during the 1950s, the population swelled to over 2,000. The Test Site itself currently employs close to 10,000 people. The medical facility was like a small community hospital, run by three doctors, two registered nurses and five paramedics during the day, and three paramedics during the swing and grave shifts. The paramedics at the facility did almost everything.

They did physical exams, sutured lacerations, put casts on broken bones, performed basic physical therapy, and administered medications. After my tour of the medical facility, I sat down in the medical administrator's office to discuss my reflections on the facility and work. The administrator's name was Stan Anson. Mr. Anson was a business administrator with no medical background. His job was to make sure that everything worked and that the bills were paid on time. He was a pleasant gentleman with a relaxed manner. I never felt inferior nor rushed during the hour-long conversation with him. He again reviewed my resume, asked about my goals and ambitions, as well as my position on nuclear energy and nuclear weapons.

At the end of the interview Stan said, "I don't have the power to directly hire you. All I can do is recommend you, but those that do the hiring, take my considerations quite seriously. So, when do you think you could start working?" I said, "Well, I'll need to give Mercy ambulance two weeks' notice." Stan smiled and said, "How does the 2nd week of July sound?" I smiled and said, "That sounds just about right." Standing up, I shook his hand and then headed back to their main office in Las Vegas.

An hour and a half later, I walked back into REECO's Human Resources office. Stan had already called ahead and told them to start the hiring process. By the time I arrived, the initial paperwork had been created and was ready for me.

I had never held a government security clearance before and was more than a little surprised by what it entailed. After reviewing the questions, I asked the personnel technician if I could have a day or two in order to get all the questions together. They wanted the addresses of every place I had ever lived. The names of neighbors that knew me at each location. The names of all my relatives, their addresses, their birthdays and social security numbers. There were 16 pages of questions. This was going to take a bit of research!

I was also a little startled when the personnel technician informed me that my first day on the job would be July 8, slightly less than two weeks away. Mercy ambulance was not going to be pleased with this news.

I wasted no time driving home and writing a nice letter of resignation. Two hours later, I pulled into Mercy's main headquarters. I sat in my car for a moment and took a deep breath. I had started working for Mercy ambulance on December 31, 1983. I had come to this town with only what would fit into my two-seater Pontiac Fierro, and a few hundred dollars to my name.

Mercy ambulance had helped me become an exceptional paramedic. With the call volume this town generated, you either got good or you burned out. I knew it was time for a change, and usually change involves a leap of faith. As I closed my car door, I thought to myself, *I hope I'm making the right decision.*

Dan Netski was the senior Mercy ambulance supervisor on duty. As I stepped into his office I said, "Hi Dan. How's your day going?" Dan grumbled, "Not too good." I said, "Well, I'm probably going to make it a lot worse." Dan looked up from his paperwork and said, "What now?" I handed him my letter and said, "Dan, I'm resigning." Dan looked as though someone had just knocked the wind out of him.

He said, "Boy, you sure know how to turn a perfectly lousy day into a really shitty one!" I sat down in the chair in front of his desk and said, "Dan, Mercy leaves me no choice. They're chewing people up and just spitting them out. When you consider the manhours and fatigue caused by this job coupled with the blatant disregard for the needs of the EMS staff, what do they expect people to do? They are turning my job into a hobby. I can't live the way I want to live on the wages and grueling hours Mercy demands. I'm the type of person that if I can't improve my status where I'm at, I'm going to go someplace where I can."

Dan said, "I can understand that, but you realize the jam that you're going to leave us in?" I said, "Dan, come on. Mercy has been losing people left and right for the past year. I think it's time they start waking up a little, because I know for a fact that if they don't, a lot more are going to leave." Dan said, "I know things aren't going well right now, but things will get better. We've got a lot of things planned for the future."

I said, "Sure, Mercy has always got a lot of things planned in the future, but nothing ever benefits the employees. Dan, Mercy netted $1 million more this year than they did the year before and yet none of the employees saw any improvement in their financial status." Dan said, "Well, I don't know about that." I said, "Seriously? You know. But you are just not allowed to say." As I stood up I said, "July 6 will be my last day as a full-time Mercy paramedic. But I'm not going to completely throw you out to dry. As I have time, I will still work part-time."

Nothing really changed my last two weeks of full-time work. In fact, I think they truly thought that if they ignored my resignation letter, I might not actually leave. Unfortunately, reality would set in all too soon.

In typical Las Vegas fashion, my last two weeks of work were extremely busy. The call volume across the city was at an all-time high, and for a change, I was running some very interesting calls.

Interestingly, I was also given a paramedic student to train. His name was Jack Weiss. Jack was from Portland, Oregon and had been assigned to several other paramedics, but wasn't getting along with them. It was no big surprise to me. They were not instructors, but burnout medics trying to make it from shift to shift. I was surprised that Jack didn't flat out quit.

Jack was thrilled to be working with a team that knew how to teach and were reasonable to be around. Jack was an excellent student and caught on quickly to how Paul and I worked. During the first few shifts we had to review the basics, but from then on, Jack was a competent, reliable third partner on our team.

During my last full-time week at Mercy, Paul took off on vacation. This allowed Jack to step up into the role as my true partner. Unfortunately, since Jack was still considered a student, we had a barrage of part-time paramedics assigned to our ambulance. In reality, Jack was my partner and the part-time paramedics acted more like the student.

We would get a call, and Jack would be doing the assessment. When he'd finish his assessment, and was ready to start his treatment, I'd have all his equipment all set up and ready to go. Everything always ran smoothly. Before Jack started working with me, I was advised by his past instructors that Jack was a slow learner, a complainer, and would probably never pass this program. Once he started working with Paul and I, he became a better partner and more enjoyable to be around than almost anyone else I'd partnered with at Mercy.

I was impressed with his ability to learn and stay cool during intense situations. That is, until we had to deliver a baby in the back of our ambulance. I had to laugh. Jack fell apart like a cheap suit, or like an expectant father.

We had received the call in the late morning hours. The woman was one-week overdue, and this was her third child. Her labor had begun about an hour before she called us, and when her labor contractions came faster than she had expected, she called us just in case she couldn't make it to the hospital.

As we responded to the call, I noticed Jack fidgeting and squirming in the back. I looked into the rearview mirror and said, "What's wrong Jack?" Jack looked up at me and said, "Man! I've never delivered a baby before." I said, "Awe, there ain't nothing to it. We probably won't have to deliver anyway."

Jack wasn't reassured. We arrived on scene to find a 30-year-old female in full labor. Her contractions were about one minute apart and lasting for about 45 seconds. Her water had already broken but she had not yet started to crown. (show the head of the baby out her vagina.) We placed her on the ambulance gurney and headed for the ambulance. Halfway from her apartment to the ambulance, she had a major contraction, resulting in her wanting to push. I rechecked her vagina and found the baby's head crowning. I said, "Jack, go open the OB kit. We're going to deliver her in the ambulance." Jack turned pale and said, "In the ambulance?" I said, "Well, it's either there or in the parking lot!" Jack hurried to the back of the ambulance to prepare for the imminent delivery.

My official partner today was Rick Kozak. Rick was a full-time Mercy paramedic that could never find a regular partner. Rick was slow, opinionated, and hard to work with. Today was my turn to tolerate him. Thank God I had Jack for backup!

Rick and I finished rolling our patient to the ambulance. Once in the back, I uncovered her and asked Rick to open a pair of sterile gloves for me. Rick was about as helpful as a bump on a log! He casually rummaged around inside of the ambulance for a pair of sterile gloves and sat in the jump seat fumbling with the package, trying to open it. The baby's head had moved past crowning to almost halfway out!

The top of the baby's head, forehead, and eyebrows were now visible. Frustrated, I said, "Rick, give me those damn gloves." I then grabbed the gloves out of Ricks hands, tore open the package, and put the gloves on just in time to help guide the baby's head out.

Jack's eyes were the size of silver dollars. I had Jack kneel beside me and instructed Jack on exactly what to do as I delivered the baby. With patience and skill, we delivered an 8 pound 4 ounce baby boy in perfect health. We then casually drove mom and her new baby boy to the hospital for a checkup and bragging rights.

This delivery marked my 18th delivery in the back of an ambulance. As we arrived to the hospital, a very nervous father greeted us at the emergency room doors. He had been so worried about his wife and unborn baby that he literally jumped for joy upon seeing both happy and healthy. While I was pleased that the delivery had gone so well, Jack was absolutely beaming. You would have thought that <u>he</u> was the father! He kept walking up to the emergency room staff saying, "This was my first! This was my first!"

As Rick and I transferred mom and baby onto the hospital gurney, mom said, "Thank you Ty for delivering my baby. As you know, this was my third child and I can't imagine a doctor doing any better job than you." I smiled and responded, "Thank you, but you did all the work! I was only there to catch."

Delivering a baby in the back of an ambulance is a messy job. It took us almost an hour to clean our ambulance and get back into service for our next call. Jack was still floating on "Cloud 9" as he came out to help clean the ambulance. "The doctor came up to me and said that we did a really good job," Jack said beaming. I just smiled and said, "Well Jack, the next one you get to deliver all by yourself."

We finished the paperwork and went back into service. The rest of the day was anti-climactic. We responded to several minor auto accidents, a seizure patient, and an attempted suicide.

The attempted suicide was somewhat unique. As we learned, a 17-year-old male had gotten into an argument with his mother and in retaliation, decided to hang himself in his bedroom. His mother had walked in to the room moments after he had kicked the chair out from underneath himself. She freaked out, ran back into the living room to call for an ambulance, and then decided that maybe she'd better cut him down. We had only been five blocks away from the house when we received the call and arrived on scene in a matter of seconds.

The mother, in the meantime, had gone back into the room and cut her son down from the ceiling. She related that he initially wasn't breathing, and she had given him mouth-to-mouth ventilations. As we arrived on scene, her son woke up, pushed her way, and ran out the back door with the yellow rope still around his neck.

We loaded our equipment onto the ambulance gurney and rushed through the front door only to find a fairly flabbergasted mother sitting in the living room crying. As she retold what had happened, the entire 7th Calvary showed up. Three Metro police squad cars, a Fire Department paramedic ambulance, and the Fire Department engine. They all came to a screeching halt in front of the house and rushing into the house armed with everything but a fire extinguisher.

Mom gave the police a description of her son, and everyone jumped back into their vehicles to start looking for a 17-year-old male wearing blue shorts and a yellow rope around his neck. I figured that if the young man could get up, jump over a 10-foot wall and head for the hills, he probably didn't need an ambulance.

Jack finished his training with Mercy ambulance with honors (in my opinion) and headed back to Oregon for his final exam. It was a rare privilege working with a paramedic partner that I found to be equal to Paul Young. At the end of our last day and shift working together,

I shook Jack's hand and said, "It's been a real pleasure, Jack. I know you will do well on your exam and I look forward to working with you at some point in the future." Jack gave me a hug and said, "I couldn't have done it without you, man." With that, he headed for his car and his home in the Pacific Northwest.

6 July, 1985

My last full-time shift at Mercy proved to be an extremely busy one. The morning started off with the typical routine of getting the ambulance stocked, check-out paperwork completed and, of course, breakfast.

During the afternoon, business picked up substantially. Around 2 PM, we received a call to a complex for a possible overdose. We were responding with an engine company, which arrived on-scene at the same time as us. As we loaded our gear onto our ambulance gurney, a firefighter called out, "He's in apartment 18. I don't know what's wrong with him. I think he's on drugs or something." I looked over at Paul and rolled my eyes. As we entered apartment 18, I noticed about six firefighters standing around in the apartment. The captain saw us enter and said, "He's here in the bathroom." Paul was attending, so he walked into the bathroom and I followed. We found an approximately 27-year-old male lying slumped over in the bathtub blue.

I initially thought the guy was dead. That is, until he made a feeble attempt to take a breath. Paul was instantly hot. Paul looked up at the group staring through the bathroom door and said, "You guys ever think about taking a first aid course?"

Paul grabbed the guy's legs and I grabbed him under the arms and we dragged him out into the living room where we could work on him more efficiently. Since I was at the head, I grabbed an Ambu bag and started ventilating the guy while Paul hooked up the oxygen and placed the patient on the cardiac monitor.

With oxygen and ventilations, the guy started to perk up. His pupils were pinpointed, which indicated he had ingested a narcotic substance. Our patient was only breathing about two times per minute on his own, so I intubated him and helped Paul set up an IV, draw blood, and institute our drug overdose protocol. There were two people in the apartment that knew the patient so Paul asked, "Has he been doing any drugs?" They both answered, "Oh no! John never did drugs!" Paul was still boiling from the lack of action by the Fire Department and he let the two friends have it with both barrels! "You're lying! What kind of drugs is he on!" The man's neighbor piped up and said, "Hey man. All he's been doing today is drinking beer and hard liquor. No drugs." Paul responded, "Well, what drugs has he done in the past?" The guy said, "Well, I wouldn't know about that." The landlady was also standing in the apartment and quipped, "He's such a nice man. He would never get involved in drugs." I drew up a syringe with 4 mg of Narcan (a drug used to counteract the effects of narcotics) and injected it intravenously into his system. John's respirations immediately started to improve, and his respiratory rate increased to 20 breaths per minute. Paul looked over his shoulder at John's friends and said, "Well, that blows your theory out of the water. You see Narcan only works on narcotics. That's its only function."

We gave John another 6 mg of Narcan (a very large dose) before he finally started to wake up.

Paul and I then secured the endotracheal tube and IV line before placing John onto the gurney and rolling him towards the ambulance. Narcan only has a therapeutic effect for about 15 to 20 minutes, and by the time we had John loaded into the ambulance, his respiratory rate and level of consciousness were starting to drop. Paul gave John another 4 mg of Narcan to bring him back around. Whatever John had taken (and no one was going to tell us), it had been quite a lot. John's buddy decided to ride to the hospital with us. He jumped into the front passenger seat with a bottle of Thunderbird. "Wrong," I said. "Let's get something straight right now, partner. Get rid of the 'T-bird' or you're not riding with me." The guy said, "Oh", and handed the bottle to the landlady. I shook my head and thought, *Why does it always happen to Paul and I?* We scooted on to the hospital and dropped John off with the emergency room staff. John was starting to become more conscious, but still wasn't really with it. We ended up having to tie him down to keep him from pulling his IV line and endotracheal tube out. While I never did find out what John took, an educated guess would be that he injected pure heroin.

A new era had come to Las Vegas society. It was called the age of "designer drugs." Chemists were finding out that they could make tons of money creating "designer drugs" for people. Nevada law stipulated that a specific illegal drug must be made from a certain chemical equation. Chemists had learned to bypass that chemical equation, but still maintain the illegal drugs effects. Let's say you take a drug like heroine; it has a certain molecular structure. If you alter that structure, even by just one molecule, it can no longer be classified as a heroine but another drug. Thus, people were getting around the illegal possession laws. The only problem with this was that if you altered the drug, you may have also altered the effects of the drug, as well as the side effects. People were finding themselves permanently disabled from experimentation with "designer drugs." I think John may have been such a candidate.

After dropping John off in the emergency room, Paul and I readied our ambulance and headed for the streets. The majority of the afternoon was filled with run-of-the-mill calls; "man down", possible seizures, possible heart attack, so on and so forth. Nothing that required more than oxygen, a heart monitor, and the occasional IV. It was turning into one of those days that simply blended into every other day working on an ambulance in Las Vegas.

The day turned into evening, and the evening to night. Paul and I had just returned to our substation when we heard Mercy Ambulance 2 (M-2) dispatched to a 401 (motor vehicle accident) at the corner of Boulder Highway and Tropicana. While they were en route, Mercy dispatch advised that there were possibly multiple patients; possibly critical. They advised that they were going to also send Mercy Ambulance 1 (M-1) for backup. Dispatch also advised that an additional Fire Department rescue squad and engine was also responding.

Paul and I decided to jump back into our ambulance and begin driving towards the scene of the accident. We had just reached Maryland Parkway when M-2 advised that additional Units were not needed. We were in the process of returning to our substation when the Nevada Highway Patrol (NHP) called back and said that, "Yes, indeed, extra Units were needed at the scene."

I looked over at Paul and said, "Now what the hell! If M-2 missed that, they're going to hear about it!" We turned around and headed back towards the accident with red lights and siren on. We decided that even if we were canceled we would continue onto the scene just to be sure.

Dispatch attempted in vain to reach M-2 for clarification of what was happening, but they never came on the radio. As we rounded the last turn in approach to the accident scene, I knew M-2 had royally screwed up. A drunk driver in a 1-ton Dodge pickup, loaded down with engine parts had blown through the intersection heading west on Tropicana. The speed and weight of the vehicle running the red light had taken out three other cars before finally coming to rest against a traffic light pole.

As I stepped out of the ambulance, one of the firefighters advised that the woman sitting sideways in the mangled Honda was dead. I stopped for a moment to look at the woman in the car, and the man beside her, still holding her hand. I turned back to the fireman and said, "Is that her husband?" He said, "Yes." I asked, "Did you tell him she's dead?" The fireman looked at me funny and said, "Well, no." I said you need to go grab a Metro officer and your captain and explain to him there's nothing we can do for her." He said, "Okay", and left to find his captain.

I looked around and saw one of the paramedics from M-2. He looked totally lost and had tunnel vision, concentrating on only one patient. His partner had done the same thing. Paul and I looked around and discovered that only four people out of the four vehicles involved had even been looked at, and that 13 had been injured including two infants, both of which were thrown against the dashboards of their respective vehicles. If it weren't for the urgency of the situation, Paul and I would've been pissed, but there was no time for that.

Paul and I decided to split up and check the remaining nine that were injured and to assume command of the mass casualty incident. Just as Paul and I began our assessments, a car pulled up containing the mother and father of the woman that had been killed. I gave a heavy sigh and thought to myself, "God, I hate having to do this."

As the parents of the dead woman approached me, another group also started walking towards me, carrying a small child, one year of age. They had seen the accident and had volunteered to watch the child of the fatally wounded mother until the ambulance crews had a chance to look at him.

Initially, the worried grandparents were concerned with the small child. I made my exam and determine the small child only had a minor bump to his head, caused by his unrestrained mother being thrown into the back seat and striking him. Such a tragedy. His mother had thought enough of him to secure him into a car seat, but not enough of herself to fasten her own seatbelt. If she would have been restrained, she'd probably be alive right now.

The main impact was on the right rear quarter panel of her vehicle. As the dead woman's parents breathed a sigh of relief that their grandchild was ok, the question that I had been dreading was asked, "Is our daughter all right?"

How do you answer questions like that? Within the next 15 seconds, a thousand responses ran through my mind; all of which sounded phony or inadequate. In that 15 seconds of silence, and in the silence of the small group around us, they knew what my answer would be. In the end, all I could say, with a tear in my eye, was, "I'm sorry."

Tears started to well up in the elderly man's eyes as he looked down at his grandson in his arms. He said, "You know, she had just found out that she was pregnant again. We were so excited about possibly having a granddaughter." I felt gutted. There was nothing I could do for this man or his family, and all I could say was "I'm sorry." I wished I could have done more.

The elderly man's wife had completely lost all strength, and collapsed to the curb sobbing uncontrollably as she looked at the wrecked vehicle. I asked the people that had been so kind to watch the young boy to stay with the couple so that I could continue to check the rest of the injured.

They graciously accepted. As I started walking to the next group of people, Paul emerged and said, "I've got them all taken care of." I asked, "What are the injuries?" Paul replied, "A lot of pissed off people for one thing. They were in two vehicles over at the center of the intersection. I was the first person to even bother to ask if they needed any help. When this call was over, there were two medics I was going to strangle." I said, "I'll help you!" Paul continued, "I treated several facial lacerations and a possible fractured arm that I splinted, and the routine back and neck pain stuff. However, because of the "dynamic duos'" fuck up, no one will ride to the hospital with us." I said, "Cute."

By this time, camera crews from every news station in town were starting to arrive. The husband of the dead woman was being consoled on the back bumper of a fire engine in plain view of his mangled wife's body. I thought to myself *Oh for Pete's sake*. I walked over to the ambulance, grabbed a sheet and covered her body before the news media realized it was there.

As I looked up from the mangled car, I saw the drunk still sitting in the front of his wrecked pickup. I yelled over to a firefighter that was standing close to him and asked, "What's wrong with him?" The firemen replied, "Oh, don't worry about him, he's got a cut on his head and one on his foot. Anyway, I think he's under arrest." The incompetency of the whole call was beginning to overwhelm me. I walked over to the intoxicated driver of the smashed pickup truck and completed an entire patient assessment, short of taking off the bandages on his head and foot.

During the exam, I determined that the guy had broken the steering wheel off with his chest and shattered both the driver's side window and the front windshield with his head. I discovered that this guy had not only been drinking, he had also been doing barbiturates. Simply put, his entire body had been anesthetized. I could have cut his arm off and he wouldn't have felt it.

I immediately immobilized the guy and extricated him onto a scoop stretcher. I had asked for a plain wooden backboard but the dippy volunteer first responder couldn't distinguish between that and an aluminum scoop stretcher. In sheer desperation, I took what he brought. I felt like I was working alone.

Finally, my patient was out and immobilized on the scoop stretcher, and secured to my ambulance gurney. With Paul's help, I loaded him into the back of my ambulance. Since I was the driver, I helped Paul get a set of vital signs and then jumped into the driver seat to transport the drunk driver to the Southern Nevada Memorial hospital.

I called the hospital and advised them that we were bringing one patient from a 401 and to notify the metro substation that he was under arrest. Once there, Dr. De Bellows began his examination of the patient. When he removed the bandages that the firemen had placed over the "little cut on his right foot," Paul and I both about fell over. The "little cut" was a severe laceration with several arterial bleeds! The small cut went all the way to the bone with an arterial bleeder as well. I felt like a fool. All I could say was, "Doc, I had no idea. Both areas were bandaged before we took over care of this patient."

This was more than Paul could take. We called dispatch and told them that we needed to speak with the on-duty supervisor immediately. Dispatch advised that the supervisor ambulance was also transporting a patient to So. Ma. Mo. and would be there any second. The on-duty supervisor was Scott Lippacher, and talking to him was like talking to a wall. He would never take action, even under the most egregious circumstances.

We waited until Scott had unloaded his patients and had given his report to the ER staff and then let him have it with both barrels. After we had finished relating what had happened, all he could say was, "I don't see what's the problem. You guys handled it, didn't you?"

Paul threw up his hands in disgust and walked out to the ambulance. I looked at Scott with disbelief and said, "You know Scott, as long as this company keeps that type of fucking attitude, it will never be more than a training ground for rookies!" I then turned around and headed out the door to my ambulance leaving Scott wondering what it was that had us pissed off.

As I opened the door and jumped into the passenger seat, Paul had it running and in reverse by the time my door closed. As we left the ambulance bay Paul began a verbal tirade, "Those God damn ignorant fucking assholes have no idea what it takes to manage an ambulance company!" I said, "I couldn't agree with you more. Just eight more hours Paul and I'll kiss this company goodbye!" Paul said, "Two more weeks and I am off for a month's vacation, and depending on how I feel, I just might not come back!" We continued to fume all the way back to our substation.

It was now 1 AM and the call volume had finally started to slow down. In the substation, I kicked off my shoes and laid down on the bed. For the first time, I realized that I was extremely tired. I tried to unwind from the events of the last couple of hours, but all I could do was think about how this drunk asshole had turned what was going to be a joyous evening for a family that had just found out they were going to have a new baby, into a hellish nightmare that will haunt them for months or even years.

I had been standing beside the drunk when the Nevada State Trooper placed him under arrest. The idiot just shook his head and laughed. Even through his drunken haze, he knew what he had done. He knew that he had killed and maimed people, yet he showed absolutely no remorse. Two people had died that night because of his actions, but he didn't even care. I later discovered that this was his third DUI bust.

In both previous accidents, he had injured other people as well. I guess this was all "old hat" to our experienced drunk. In my eyes, he was a habitual offender, a felon that had no place in my society. I never wanted to see him out on the street again and capable of killing me or one of my friends. I asked one of the state troopers how much time he'd spend in jail. He told me a mandatory six years, plus whatever the judge throws at him.

People have the tendency to think that Nevada State Troopers are real jerks, but I like their style and way of thinking. They believe that if they treat you sternly, and make every traffic stop a stern and perhaps unpleasant experience, just maybe it would keep folks from screwing up further down the road.

Some of these troopers can get downright severe; take for instance the Trooper dealing with our drunk. The Trooper was a good friend of mine. I said, "Terry, this guy was formally placed under arrest at the scene, but I don't think he knows that he killed people." Terry said, "He doesn't does he? Well, I'll just have to tell him."

Officer Terry walked into the room where the drunk lay waiting to be sutured. His family was also in the room. His brother, mom, dad, and girlfriend. I had personally allowed all of them into the room just so that they could hear what Terry was about to say. The drunk's name was Lester. Terry started in, "Lester, I was in at the scene when you were placed under arrest, and I just want to make sure you know what you're being arrested for." Lester broke in with a half-assed smile and said, "Yeah, yeah I know, drinking and driving." Terry said, "Not quite. You are under arrest for felony DUI. That means that someone was either seriously injured or killed and in this case, both." Terry continued on and reread him his Miranda rights and then finished off with, "Lester, I understand that this isn't the first time you've been arrested on DUI charges. I hope you like cement and Barb wire. You're going to be seeing a lot of it soon."

Lester's family and friends had initially been whispering and giggling in the corner. They now stood speechless, pale and decidedly upset. I stood in the corner watching the setup unfold. Terry then turned to me and said, "Well Ty, I've got to be going. I'll see you in court when we put this one behind bars." I looked over Lester and our eyes met as I responded to Terry, "With pleasure my friend, with pleasure."

It was past 2 o'clock in the morning before I finally drifted off to sleep. As I heard Paul toss and turn several times in his bed across the room I figured he too was having a tough time sleeping.

Thankfully, the final hours of the shift were non-productive. We were called out of bed at 3 AM, 5 AM, and 7 AM.

Each time, we were canceled several blocks away from the scene. When 8 o'clock rolled around, both Paul and I were ready to go home and sleep.

7 July, 1985

I drove home and took a shower to wash the grime of the past shift off my body, and tried to rinse the distressing thoughts of that horrible accident out of my mind. While fatal accidents are horrible tragedies, they should also be moments when paramedics shine the brightest. My peers working on M-2 missed that opportunity to be beacons of light to those experiencing probably one of the darkest moments in their lives. They blew it. Paul and I did what we could to make up for their inequities, but I felt it wasn't enough.

As I laid down in my bed preparing to sleep, the sights, sounds, and smells of that accident kept rolling through my mind. I was still replaying the scene in my mind, when the telephone rang. It was Robin Nunn on the other end. She was working at Mercy dispatch and said, "How long will it take for you to put on a Mercy uniform and get down here. We just had a mass casualty incident (MCI) at one of the hotels downtown."

I gave a heavy sigh. I was very upset with Mercy ambulance management, but I would never say no to the people of Las Vegas during a time of disaster. I said, "About 15 minutes. Why? What happened." "A water heater malfunctioned and had been leaking carbon monoxide gas throughout most of the hotel. Two people died and I'm not sure how many more are affected." I said, "I'll be right down." I threw on a Mercy uniform and sped down to station one. An ambulance was waiting for me. As soon as I jumped into the passenger seat, we were off on an emergency call downtown.

It amazed me how I could go months running routine, run-of-the-mill calls and then have a 24 hour shift that was full of some of the most memorable calls of my career. The past 24-36 hours was shaping up to be one of those times.

Dispatch felt that they had enough Units at the hotel incident, but still needed help covering the rest of the city. So while other Units responded to the mass casualty incident, Bill Smith and I were saving lives throughout the rest of the city. The first call out of the station was at the First Federal Bank for a "man-down" which turned out to be nothing more than a feisty old transient that had fallen asleep inside the bank on a lobby bench, and didn't take kindly to being woken up.

Our next call also came under the classification of "man-down." This time, however, it was to the transient rescue mission. Our patient was an alcoholic, who had lost all his money in a poker game and was now going into D.T's (delirium tremens) from not having much to eat or drink in the last couple of days.

As the calls progressed, the exhaustion of the past 36 hours began to catch up with me. I had initially been pumped up with adrenaline in preparation for responding to another mass casualty incident. By noon, I was having an extremely hard time staying awake, yet the call volume wasn't slowing down enough to allow us to go home. We continued to run calls in the downtown area. Most of them were for seizures or fainting related incidents. In my exhaustion, they all blended together.

By 3pm, the call volume had finally slowed enough to let us go home. By this time, I was definitely ready to go to sleep. I drove home, turned the phone ringer off, and fell fast asleep.

Tomorrow would be a busy day.

It would be my first day at the Nevada Nuclear Test Site, and the start of chapter 1, page 1 of a new diary entitled, "The Secret Diary of a Nuclear Test Site Medic."

ABOUT THE AUTHOR

Ty W.K. Flewelling, PA-C
Medical Attaché

Ty Flewelling is the U.S. Department of State's Clinical Director of Medevac Center Operations in Pretoria, South Africa. He is a Physician Assistant, Board Certified in Primary Care and Surgery. As a career U.S. Foreign Service Diplomat, he has spent the past twenty years providing healthcare to U.S. Embassies in Ashgabat Tashkent, Ankara Turkey, Santo Domingo Dominican Republic, Maputo Mozambique, Tel Aviv Israel, and Pretoria South Africa. He has also served as the Deputy Director in the Office of Medical Clearances in Washington D.C.

Prior to joining the Department of State, Mr. Flewelling was a Peace Corps Medical Officer in Ashgabat Turkmenistan, and the Deputy Director of the Navajo Nation Health Foundation - Emergency Department.

Mr. Flewelling started his medical career as a Paramedic, working for both ground and air EMS services in Iowa, Nevada, Wyoming, New Mexico and Florida. He is married with three children.

Made in the USA
Monee, IL
23 December 2020

55467004R00142